THE WASPS

The Complete Greek Comedy
Edited by William Arrowsmith

Aristophanes

The Wasps

Translated by Douglass Parker

with sketches by Geraldine Sakall

Ann Arbor

The University of Michigan Press

Published in the United States of America by
The University of Michigan Press and simultaneously
in Toronto, Canada, by Ambassador Books Limited

Library of Congress Catalog Card No. 62-13450

Manufactured in the United States of America
by The Haddon Craftsmen, Inc., Scranton 9, Pa.
Designed by George Lenox

PARENTIBUS SUIS

HAS LITTERAS

PRO EPISTULIS

INTERPRES

D. D. D.

CONTENTS

Introduction   1

The Wasps   9

Notes   119

Glossary   125

Introduction

The Play   *The Wasps* is not a favorite of modern readers. For two-thirds of its length, its subject matter is felt to be obscure except to specialists, while the final third concludes in a fashion that even specialists lament as unconnected, or else try to explain away on the grounds of a built-in flaw in the form of Old Comedy. The first of these objections can be met with a brief explanation: Athenian law, a far different entity than modern American law, found its characteristic judicial expression in courts where guilt and, on occasion, sentence were decided by the majority vote of huge juries, sometimes composed of as many as 1001 citizens. These dicasts (a word which may be glossed, in view of their functions, by either "judges" or "jurors") were daily chosen to serve from the six thousand citizens who constituted the annual panel. Before the mid-fifth century, dicasts performed this service gratis, but Perikles instituted a small salary, probably in 462, and the demagogue Kleon increased it to three obols per man per jury day in 425 or 424. The buying power of this amount cannot be firmly expressed in modern equivalents; it could pay for a pigeon, or three salted fish, or the cleaning of a cloak. In any case, it was barely enough to sustain life in a small family, and, as a result, jury duty seems to have attracted mainly those who had no other income or chance of any. Primarily the old. Such a system does not necessarily contain within itself the assurance of justice to all; to a conservative playwright, however, the case was clear and fast: the jurors were inevitably the creatures of Kleon and the other demagogues to whom they owed their pay, and were further, because of their poverty, fair game for bribery.

It was with an attack on this state of affairs that Aristophanes returned to political comedy at the Lenaia of 422, offering *The Wasps*. Here the protagonist, old Philokleon the demon dicast, is weaned from his boss-ridden, jury-going ways by his virtuous son, Phobokleon (as here translated), with successive applications of force, logic, and what we might call therapy—the home trial of a dog for stealing the cheese. At length, a full cure from litigiousness is effected—and 500 lines still remain in the play.

Which brings us to the second objection to *The Wasps*. What is the ending doing there, anyway? Why the long scene in which Phobokleon attempts to make his father a gentleman, the wild drunk scene with the nude flute-girl, the utterly unrelated dance? To those who regard Aristophanes as a pamphleteer, the answer is either clumsiness (he was, after all, still young) or a [necessary] constraint inherent in the form ("every Old Comedy must end with wild farce and a festive procession"), coupled with a not-too-laudable desire to please the groundlings. More perceptive critics attempt to see the play as a whole, and sometimes offer a line from Horace in summation of the plot: *Naturam expellas furca, tamen usque recurret*—roughly rendered, "You can't fight human nature." Philokleon reformed is worse than Philokleon the unreconstructed juryman.

Now, this is good, so far as it goes, but it stops short of a final solution. Behind the judging attacked in *The Wasps* we can see another judgment festering, the judgment which the year before had rejected Aristophanes' favorite child, his comedy of ideas, *The Clouds*. The extensive revision of the earlier play has not prevented critics from noting the basic similarity of the two comedies. In both, the protagonist changes his ways under the force of instruction to the point where he completely reverses his former behavior. But in *The Clouds*, the instruction was in what Aristophanes regarded, let us say, as a vice; in *The Wasps* it is in virtue—and the result is hopeless. This is more than a simple warping of the plot; it is an inversion: both the moral and the aesthetics set forth in the Grand Experiment of 423 are flung down and, quite literally, danced upon. Further, we have an obvious allegory, rather more thoroughgoing than usual. Philokleon, the litigious old man, has obvious affinities with Demos, the "Uncle Sam" of *The Knights,* and is the Athenian people viewed in the practice of its characteristic weakness; Phobokleon—the young reformer, the idealist with purely altruistic motives, the Kleon-hater who is thereby accused of subversive antidemocratic leanings—is Aristophanes himself; and the play is a dramatic presentation of what he sets forth explicitly in the Parabasis—the failure of his teaching to change his fellow-citizens for the better.

Indeed, the whole play is a calculated insult to the audience's intelligence. Not only does it break every rule of good comedy formulated by Aristophanes in *The Clouds* 537 ff. (though this may have been written later), but it contradicts its own program, expounded by Xanthias in lines 57-63. We have an avowedly slapstickless play that wallows in knockabout farce; a professedly nonpolitical play whose principals are "Kleon-Lover" and "Kleon-Hater"; a play which avoids attacking Euripides by bringing him on stage (so I believe) in an advanced stage of disrepair; a chaste play whose Chorus is distinguished by a phallic peculiarity. And so forth. And, in the final wild dance, Philokleon, once juryman, now jury-bait, has progressed from Phrynichos the elder to Phrynichos the younger, has been rejuvenated according to comic formula—and still prefers indecent spectacle to sense. His triumph in the dance is his defeat as a rational being. Aristophanes, with an overt contempt for his audience's taste rarely matched elsewhere (the Introduction to Ben Jonson's *Bartholomew Fair* affords some comparison), has given the people what they want—and, in giving, damned them for wanting.

But there is one more turn of the screw. Happily ignorant of the present-day criticism which damns his *dramatis personae* as a clutch of two-dimensional types, Aristophanes has complicated his characters beyond mere allegory, however ironic. Philokleon is more than the Old Reprobate, more than a symbol of Athens' excesses—he is violently himself. Utterly immoral, completely loveless, distinguished by the most thoroughgoing lack of *sophrosune* in Greek drama, he is yet driven to his reprehensibilities by a fierce inner integrity which is somehow wholly admirable. He knows who he is, and will prove it in any environment, at any cost. And does, over and over again. Opposite him is his son Phobokleon—the voice of the author, his virtues undoubted, altruistic to his father's selfishness. More fundamental, however, is a much less admirable form of altruism: Phobokleon is, at bottom, a snob; his virtues are not self-impelled, but generated *ad hoc* by his concern for appearances, for the good opinion of the Right People. He is no hypocrite, but his basic inadequacy blooms after the Parabasis, when, having achieved the Good Life for his father, he can only define it as the approved paradise of those rakehells who comprise his peer-group. In one sense, then, our choice lies between doing the right things for the wrong reason (Phobokleon) and doing the wrong things for the right reason (Philokleon). Not an easy choice, and the despair of the seeker after black and white—but an intensely comic polarity.

Thus is irony ironized beyond pamphleteering, incident endowed with the cross-welter of meanings, the coexistence of mutual exclusives, which marks great drama of any sort. Aristophanes has expanded his pique at the failure of *The Clouds* into a funny play, and counterpointed it into a fine one. It would be satisfying to report to lovers of poetic justice that this play carried off the first prize, but such does not seem to be the case. The account of the competition is confused, but it would appear that Aristophanes entered two plays at the Lenaia of 422, and defeated his *Wasps* with his *Rehearsal*. Poetic justice is rarely simple.

The Wasps, with its scholia, is our greatest single source of knowledge for the minute workings of the Athenian jury system—but this translation is not. Had Aristophanes written a didactic *De Iuris Natura* in Greek, the translator's aim would be, of course, to reproduce it; but he wrote a comedy, and nothing kills comedy or poetry like a niggling antiquarianism. Thus, with the initial statement above concerning the basic difference between Athenian and American jury practice, I consider the reader prepared; other significant facts can be gained from the text, where necessary intruded glosses have, on a very few occasions, been amplified by notes. Points of little or no importance for the appreciation and understanding of the play have been swallowed up in modern analogues and legal diction. In this connection, I have regretfully kept at a minimum Latin, still even in America the hallmark of the law. No translator of Aristophanes can avoid anachronism, or wants to, but there are limits.

For the rest, the principles stated in the Introduction to *The Acharnians* apply, with a few additional observations. *The Wasps* is not a play which depends vitally on rhetorical tension and contrast, and expansion in that line is much less here. On the other hand, stage directions, or intruded glosses to supplant them, are much more common, as befits a play in which the slapstick element is quite large. Unison choruses—to state a principle which applies to *The Acharnians* as well—should be conceived of as *sung, not chanted,* and, in the unlikely event of production, music should be provided. The modern rendition of stasima via that bastard form of noncommunication known as Choral Speaking may impart a bogus patina of ritual to tragedy, but has no conceivable excuse for appearing in a comedy.

A word on staging. The proscenium stage requires the entrance of the Chorus from the wings, an entrance which I have thus tried to slow down; the motivation is not far to seek, happily. The house has inevitably been located center stage, in the Greek fashion, though there is little *dramatic* reason for this. Further consideration has brought me to conclude that it might with profit be located at the left, with the Chorus making its entrance from the right. This would allow freer movement on a modern stage. In any event, the Chorus' presence on stage is felt, if not seen, from its initial appearance until the play's end. One other suggestion should be noted: the front door might possess a wicket, or some such device, through which Philokleon can be seen when necessary.

Though my basic text has been Coulon's (1924), supplemented by Cantarella's (1954), I have made so many minor changes, particularly in line assignments, that it would be pointless to record them. I wish, however, to set down my demurral at one triumph of modern scholarship: both Coulon and Cantarella, out of obscure fealty to Wilamowitz, to that will-of-the-wisp called the "Three-Actor Law," and to a woolly-brained scholiast with pretensions to literary criticism, refuse to name the principal slaves, and deny the "First Servant" (i.e., Sosias) any independent utterance after line 137, giving the balance of the slave speeches in the opening scene to the "Second Servant" (i.e., Xanthias), who also receives every word of lines 54-135. I refuse, for my part, to share in the fruits of this victory of method over intelligence; I have gone back to earlier texts, picked and chosen, and reinstated Sosias at the expense of the "Second Servant" or "A Servant" in several places, notably 1292 ff. At least one slave in *The Wasps* has a well-defined character: he is a coward and a blusterer—and his name, in this version, is Sosias. In this connection, my adoption of Van Leeuwen's *oise* for the MSS *Chroise* (Wilamowitz *Kroise*) should be noted at 1251. Other important deviations are commented on as they occur. I have derived aid and comfort—and an occasional pun—from the editions of Starkie (1897), Rogers (2d. ed., 1915), and Van Leeuwen (2d. ed., 1909).

Acknowledgments   Again, gratitude is due the University of California, for typing grants; Donna Lippert, for typing; the indefatigable triumvirate of Donald Johns, William Sharp, and Marshall Van Deusen, for perceptive patience. More inexpressible thanks fall to William Arrowsmith, for his thoroughgoing, masterful critiques and his healthy, bracing differences of opinion (some of them not resolved at this writing); and to my wife, not only for putting up with all this, but for putting in her three obols' worth, time and again, to my great profit. I am especially in the debt of the Welsh poet Will Fletcher, who has helped me more than, under the circumstances, he can ever know.

DOUGLASS PARKER

Characters of the Play

SOSIAS } *Slaves of Phobokleon*
XANTHIAS }

PHOBOKLEON, *son of Philokleon*

PHILOKLEON, *an elderly Athenian juror*

FIRST KORYPHAIOS

SECOND KORYPHAIOS

CHORUS *of elderly Athenian Jurors* (*WASPS*)

FIRST LITTLE BOY

SECOND LITTLE BOY

FLEAHOUND, *a dog*

CHOWHOUND, *a dog*

A FLUTE-GIRL

A BANQUET GUEST

MYRTIA, *proprietress of a bakery*

CHAIREPHON

THE MAN WHO LOOKS LIKE EURIPIDES

A WITNESS

SLAVES

ASSORTED KITCHEN UTENSILS

PUPPIES

OUTRAGED GUESTS AND SMALL TRADESMEN

THREE SONS OF KARKINOS

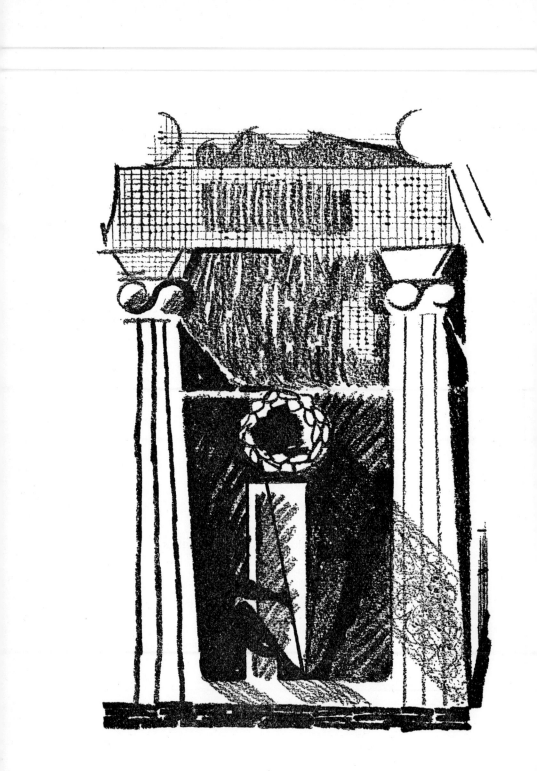

SCENE: *A street in Athens. In the background, center, the house of Philokleon and Phobokleon, a two-storied dwelling with a front door, a side door, and a second-story window. A huge net covers the entire façade, draped so that the doors are free. Over the front door, a wreath. Phobokleon is asleep on the flat roof. On guard before the house, armed with long iron spits, are the two slaves, Sosias and Xanthias. They are very weary. Xanthias, in fact, is asleep. The time is shortly before dawn.*

SOSIAS

Shaking Xanthias.

Xanthias!

No answer. He shakes again.

What the hell do you think you're doing?

XANTHIAS

I'm studyin'. How to Relieve the Watch. One easy lesson.

He goes back to sleep.

SOSIAS

You're aching for trouble. Have you forgotten what we're guarding? A MONSTER!

XANTHIAS

Scares me so much

I'm afraid to stay awake.

Back to sleep again.

SOSIAS

Okay, it's your neck. . . .
Go ahead, see if I care. . . . Why should I care?
I can hardly keep *my* eyes open.

He snuggles down.

Delicious!

He goes to sleep; then, after a moment or two of silence, begins to thrash around wildly, kicking Xanthias awake.

XANTHIAS

Now what? Have you gone crazy? Or did you join those holy-rolling Asiatic Korybants?*

SOSIAS

Neither.
But it *was* a divine visitation. *And* from Asia.
Bacchos descended and filled me with his presence.
He produces a wine bottle and drinks. Xanthias,
after a look, produces his bottle and drinks.

XANTHIAS

A fellow-worshipper! The real afflatus—Phrygian
liquid sleep. One thing about Oriental religion—
it's *restful.*

He drinks again.

Except, it made me dream just now—
incredible!

SOSIAS

Me, too. A highly abnormal nightmare. . . .
You tell yours first.

XANTHIAS

I seemed to see an eagle
swoop down, massive and vast, upon the city,
clench in his claws a brazen buckler, bear it
aloft to heaven—
and turn into Kleonymos, and throw
the shield away.

SOSIAS

Say what you want about Kleonymos,
he's a wonderful riddle.

XANTHIAS

How so?

SOSIAS

It can win you a drink:
"What animal defends itself by shedding its armor?"

XANTHIAS

That dream—what an omen!

SOSIAS

Don't worry. It can't mean anything
disastrous.

10

XANTHIAS

        Kleonymos can't mean anything *but*.
—It's your turn; you tell your dream.

SOSIAS

                        Mine's a big one.
It concerns the whole hull of the Ship of State.

XANTHIAS

Then get a move on, man, and lay the keel.

SOSIAS

I'd no sooner gone to sleep than I dreamed about sheep,
all members of the Assembly, meeting on the Pnyx. *Dressed* sheep—
they all were carrying canes and wearing cloaks.
Up front, I saw a greedy, rapacious whale
haranguing these poor sheep in a booming bellow,
the bloated blatting of a swollen sow.

XANTHIAS

                Pew!

SOSIAS

What's wrong?

XANTHIAS

        You can stop right there. Whales, sows—
your nightmare stinks of rotten leather; it reeks
of that tanner Kleon.*

SOSIAS

        Then this filthy whale
took up a bag and filled it with lumps of fat.

XANTHIAS

Oh, god, it *is* Kleon! He's sacking Greece!

SOSIAS

Squatting on the ground beside the whale
I saw Theoros. He had a crow's head. At least,
that's what *I* said it was. But Alkibiades—he was
in my dream—*he* said Theoros was a sapsucker.*
Alkibiades isn't much on birds.

XANTHIAS

Maybe not.
He *is* a pretty good judge of character, though.

SOSIAS

But isn't that mysterious, Theoros turning into a crow?

XANTHIAS

No mystery at all. Best thing that could happen.

SOSIAS

How?

XANTHIAS

How? He's a man, then suddenly he becomes a crow—
the interpretation's obvious. Your dream means that Theoros
will soar away from us—

SOSIAS

And what?

XANTHIAS

—and CROAK!*

*He ducks as Sosias, disgusted, swings wildly,
then picks up the two iron spits and chases him
around the stage.*

SOSIAS

Stop, you subtle soothsayer! Come here, you two-bit
prophet—I want to give you your pay: two spits!

XANTHIAS

Hold it! Let me tell the audience the plot.
The chase stops. He turns to the audience.

First, Gentlemen, a few preliminary remarks.
Don't look for anything too high-brow from us;
or for any slapstick smuggled out of Megara.
We haven't got those two slaves chucking chestnuts
out of a basket to keep the audience happy,
or Herakles to be swindled out of his supper again.
As for the aesthetic bit—that's out. We won't
bring on Euripides to get another working over.
Now Kleon's illustrious, thanks to luck*—no matter,
we won't chop him up into hash *again:* No Politics.

We merely have a little plot with a moral—
not too refined and dainty for *you,* of course,*
but rather more intelligent than smutty farce.
So look—

Pointing at Phobokleon.

that's our master there—asleep
topside—the big fellow—the one up on the roof.
He's locked his father indoors, and set us two
on sentry duty so the old man can't go out.
The father's sick with a baffling, unnatural disease,
so strange that none of you would ever guess it
unless I told you . . .

Listening to some imaginary voice from the audience.

You don't believe me? Try it!

Listening again and pointing.

There's Pronapes' son Amynias.—You say the old man's
sick with *dice*-addiction?

SOSIAS*

Dice-addiction!
He's judging from his own disease. —Dead wrong, Amynias!

XANTHIAS

Not quite.—Take fifty per cent, Amynias. Addiction
is half of the affliction.

*Jerking a thumb at Sosias, who is beckoning
to someone in the audience.*

Sosias is telling Derkylos
the old man's addicted to *drink.*

SOSIAS

I certainly am not!
That's a gentleman's disease. What would *he* know about it?

XANTHIAS

Pointing again.

You have a theory, Nikostratos? He's a *sacrifice*-addict—
a religious fanatic? No. Oh, then you say
he's a *hospitality*-addict?

SOSIAS

You mean like Philoxenos, the Perfect
Host? Perfect to a fault—he's a bugger. NO!

14

XANTHIAS
To the audience in toto.

> These feeble guesses are futile—you'll never find out.
> If you really want to know, then quiet down,
> and I'll tell you the master's disease in just a minute.

He pauses and waits for silence.

> He's a JURY-addict! Most violent case on record.
> He's wild to render verdicts, and bawls like a baby
> if ever he misses a seat on the very first bench.
> He doesn't get any sleep at night, not a wink.
> Or, if he closes his eyes a speck, he's in Court—
> all night his mind goes flapping around the water-clock.
> You know those pebbles that the Jurors drop into the urns
> marked *Guilty* and *Not Guilty,* to record their votes on the verdict?
> Well, he's squeezed *his* pebble so often and so hard
> that when he wakes up, he has three fingers stuck together,
> like someone putting incense on the festival altar.
> And worse. Let him see the name of a fathead faggot
> scrawled on a wall—*"I letch for Demos; he's a doll"*—
> and he scratches beside it, *"I itch for the Jury; it's a jewel."*
> Once his rooster didn't crow till sundown. Know
> what he said? "That cock's corrupt! The officials under investigation
> bribed him to wake me up too late for Court!"
> Now he shouts for his shoes right after supper;
> he's over there *way* before dawn, and goes to sleep
> clutching a courtroom column just like a barnacle.
> And nasty—watch him in action! When he takes his tablet
> to fix the penalty, he always draws the Long Line:*
> everyone gets the maximum sentence from him!
> Then off for home like a bee—or a *bumble*-bee—
> wax just plastered underneath his fingernails.
> He's petrified that he might run out of those pebbles
> he uses for voting; so he keeps a *beach* in the house.
> In sum, he's insane; the more we reason with him,
> the more he judges everybody else. Absolutely
> hopeless. Incurable.

> So now we've locked him up
> with bolts, and watch to be sure he doesn't go out.
> The son, you see, takes his daddy's disease quite hard.
> First, he tried the Word Cure. Gently he wheedled
> and pleaded the old man to put away his cloak
> and stay home.

Didn't work. So next, the Water Cure.
Dunked him and dosed him.
No dice.
Then Applied Religion.
Made him a Korybant.
Tambourine and all, his daddy
banged his way into court for more drumhead justice.
Finally, as a last recourse, he turned to Pure Prayer.
One night he grabbed the old man, sailed over to Aigina,
and bedded him down for the cure in Asklepios' temple . . .
and up he popped at dawn by the jury-box gate!
Since then, we never let him out of the house.
At first, he kept sneaking out the pipes and drains
and running away. And so we plugged up all
the holes with hunks of rag, and sealed them tight.
He reacted rather like a jackdaw—kept banging pegs
in the wall, running down, and hopping off.
At last we took these nets and draped them around
all over the house—and *now* we keep him in.
One more thing about the old man—he's a KLEON-addict!
—I mean it! That's his name, in fact: PHILOKLEON!
His son takes the opposite tack. In this and everything.
He *hates* Kleon. And that's *his* name: PHOBOKLEON!*
He's sort of a snooty, snorty, holier-than-thou-er . . .

PHOBOKLEON

Awake.

Xanthias! Sosias! You asleep?

XANTHIAS

Oh-oh!

SOSIAS

What's up?

XANTHIAS
Phobokleon.

PHOBOKLEON
Pointing at the side door.
One of you get over here right away!
Xanthias obeys.

Father's gone and got into the stove. He squeaked in
somehow, and now he's skittering around like a mouse.
—*You* see that he doesn't slip out the bathtub drain.
Sosias runs to the house.
—*You* keep leaning on that door.

XANTHIAS
                                        Yessir! Yessir!
*Silence. Then the trapdoor on the chimney is
slowly raised from within.*

PHOBOKLEON
Almighty Poseidon, what's that creaking in the chimney?
*Philokleon's head begins to emerge cautiously
from the chimney.*
        Hey, who are you?

PHILOKLEON
                        I'm smoke, and I'm issuing forth.

PHOBOKLEON
Smoke? That's nice. What wood are you from?

PHILOKLEON
                                        I'm peach wood.*
*He starts to clamber out. Phobokleon shoves
him back.*

PHOBOKLEON
Impeacher-wood? Too acrid. Back you go!
*He shoves Philokleon all the way back into the
chimney, and slams the trapdoor over the opening,
then lifts a large log over it.*
        Peace to your ashes. I'm putting the damper down—
        with a log on top. Think up another one.
He drops the log on the chimney with a crash.
        I don't have troubles enough—now I'll be famous—
        son of a smudgepot, a smokestack for my family tree!
The front door shakes violently.

SOSIAS
Somebody at the door.

PHOBOKLEON
                         Push hard! Squeeze tightly!
Show what you're made of!
The slaves strain against the front door.
                                        I'll be down and help you.
Watch out—keep an eye on that door bar. You know what he's like.
He'll probably chew the nut right off the bolt.
He disappears into the house.

PHILOKLEON
From behind the locked front door.
What are you up to? Damn you, let me out to judge!
Do you want Drakontides to be *acquitted?*

SOSIAS
                                        Would that bother you?

PHILOKLEON
BOTHER? The oracle at Delphoi warned me once:

"Thy first acquittal bringeth thy final summons!"

SOSIAS
Apollo preserve us from prophecies like that one!
*Phobokleon emerges from the side door and puts
his shoulder to the front door.*

PHILOKLEON
Please let me out—I'll bust!

PHOBOKLEON
                                The answer is NO!

PHILOKLEON
Then I'll—I'll gnaw the net through with my teeth!

PHOBOKLEON
You don't *have* any teeth.

PHILOKLEON
                        Consarn it all!
How can I kill you? How? Give me my sword!
Or—quick! Bring me a tablet—I'll *sentence* you!

PHOBOKLEON
I'm afraid the old man's plotting something desperate.

PHILOKLEON
Me? I wouldn't think of it.
                              I only want
to bring the donkey out and sell him. That's all.
It's market day, you know.

PHOBOKLEON
                              Oh, come, now. *I*
can sell the donkey.

PHILOKLEON
                    Not as good as *I* can!

PHOBOKLEON
Better, by god!

PHILOKLEON
                    Will you *please* let the donkey out?

SOSIAS
He's a slippery old cuss. And talk about excuses!
Just to get out of the house!

PHOBOKLEON
                              And what good did it do?
All that angling and not a single bite.
Still, I'd better go in and get that donkey;
we can't have Papa popping out again.
He unbars the door, enters the house, and leads out
the donkey. Philokleon is hanging underneath it,
as Odysseus hung under the Kyklops' ram, face up,
but has miscalculated a little; his head is directly
under the donkey's rear. The donkey appreciates
this not at all, and hee-haws piteously.
                    Packass, why all the tears? Don't you *want* to be sold?
Get a move on!
The donkey stands stock-still and bawls louder.
                              Why all the noise? Are you carrying
an Odysseus—something like that?

SOSIAS

Peeking under the donkey and espying Philokleon.

By god, he *is!*
One of those snuck under him right back here!

PHOBOKLEON

What's that? Let me see.

—There he is, all right. What *is* this?
Pardon me, sir, but who might you be?

PHILOKLEON

Nobody.

PHOBOKLEON

Nobody? Hmmm. From what country?

PHILOKLEON

Ithaka. Son of
Skedaddle.

PHOBOKLEON

A likely story. Well, Nobody, no bloody
fun for you!

To Sosias.

Drag him out of there! Hurry!

*As Philokleon's head emerges from between the
donkey's rear legs.*

That old dunghill—of all the places to hide!
what do I tell my friends?

"Oh, that old foal
is my father. He's the biggest man in the Borough."

PHILOKLEON

Clinging to the donkey and fending off Sosias.
You let me alone, or there's going to be a fight!

PHOBOKLEON

You'll have to fight us both—what's so important?

PHILOKLEON

I'll lose my ass!

He is dragged out.

PHOBOKLEON

You're rotten—all tricks and no scruples.

PHILOKLEON

Rotten? Me? You're badly mistaken, son.
Why, a man like me's just at his tastiest—well hung,
right in my prime. Wait till you see the stake
I'm going to leave you.

PHOBOKLEON

Take that ass and shove it—
and yourself—back in the house!

PHILOKLEON
As he and the donkey are forced back in.

Help!
Colleagues! Jurors! Kleon! Somebody!
HALP!

PHOBOKLEON
Slamming the door shut after Philokleon.

Shout to your heart's content—this door stays locked!
—Sosias, pile lots of rocks against the door—
then stick the pin back into the bar again,
and shove the beam against *that*. Then both of you
find that bowl—the huge one—and roll it up.
And please show a little speed!
*The slaves obey in a flurry of action. Suddenly
Sosias, near the house, gives a jump.*

SOSIAS

Ouch! They got me!
*Rubbing his head, as the others turn to him
increduously.*

Honestly—some plaster hit me!
Where'd it come from?

XANTHIAS
There's probably a mouse up there. *It* hit you.

SOSIAS
Looking up.

A mouse?
Up where?

22

Philokleon's head appears at the edge of the roof.
                         That's no mouse.

                              But I see something
          that tunneled under the tiles.
To Phobokleon.

                              You'd better hurry
          and sell this house, Boss—it's got *Jurors!*

          PHOBOKLEON
Seeing his father.

                                        Again?
          Why do these things happen to me? Now he's a sparrow,
          all set to fly away! Where did I put that net?
*He grabs a long-handled net and waggles
it at Philokleon.*
          Shoo! Back in there! Shoo!
*Philokleon's head disappears. Phobokleon looks
around hopelessly.*
                              I swear to god,
          I'd rather be up north with the army, and freeze
          myself blue, blockading Skione, than try
          to keep this idiot father of mine at home.

          SOSIAS
          Well, I guess we've scared him off for good.
          All the holes are plugged—he can't sneak out.
          What about a nap?
Phobokleon frowns at him.
                         Not a *long* one—
He produces his bottle again.

                                   just a—
          just a drop?

          PHOBOKLEON
                    Are you crazy? Father's friends are coming—
          the other Jurors! In just a minute or two,
          they'll be along to summon him.

          SOSIAS

                                   A minute or two?
          It won't be light for an hour!

PHOBOKLEON

                              I know. They must
have got up late today. They usually stagger by
this street just at midnight, carrying lamps.
They summon father by mumbling and moaning those ancient,
sticky-sweet, Asiatic songs by Phrynichos.*

SOSIAS

                                    So?
It's just a bunch of old men—what's the worry?
If they make any ruckus, we can throw a few rocks.
That'll shake them up.

PHOBOKLEON

                         This is *not* "just a bunch of old men,"
you cretin! These are authentic Athenian Jurors,
choked with pride, crammed with spleen and venom.
Shake *them* up, anger *them*—and you'll discover
you've annoyed a nest of maddened wasps.
                                  A sting,
keen and sharp, projects from each one's loins.
When they're aroused, they spring with wild cries
and sting, and jump, and judge like fiery sparks.

He returns to the roof.

SOSIAS

I say don't worry. Give me my rocks, and I
can eradicate any wasps' nest—jurors or not.

*In spite of Phobokleon's injunctions, he and the two
slaves go to sleep almost immediately—and, as
will appear, quite soundly. A short pause, and the
Chorus of Wasps—that is, of Old Men who sit on
juries—staggers on. They are divided into two
Semichoruses, each led by a Koryphaios and a
little boy with a lamp. They wear tattered cloaks
and, in the place of the normal comic phalluses,
enlarged representations of wasps' stings.* Their
chief characteristic is age: they are impossibly old
and crabbed, and walk bent, scanning the ground,
in a painful shuffle that contrasts sharply with
the exhortations of the First Koryphaios.*

FIRST KORYPHAIOS

Forward, boys—brisk's the word!

*To one dodderer who is not moving appreciably
slower than the rest.*

Hey, Komias, you're dragging!
Once you whipped us along. Now look at you—rotten leather.
Charinades here makes better time!

To the Second Koryphaios.

Hey, there, Strymodoros!
Euergides—did he make it? Did Chabes come in from Phlya?

SECOND KORYPHAIOS

They're all here—the last of the Boys of the Old Brigade.

He stops, lost in reminiscence.

Byzantion—how long ago? Why, it's nearly fifty years!
And what a wild bunch we were! Remember that baker's wife?
You and I, we went halves. We slipped off watch and split her
breadboard up for kindling. Mad?—Those were the days!

FIRST KORYPHAIOS

Fine, fine—but let's hurry to Court!

—Put some muscle in it!
Laches gets it today! He's up for survey. They say
he's loaded—got pots of money—squeezed Sicily dry.*
And the Boss—Kleon—was mighty insistent yesterday:
"Be EARLY!" he said. "Bring a triple ration of ANGER!" he said.
"Whatever you do, CONVICT that criminal!"—That's what he said.
So we'd better rush and be there, boys, before it gets light.

SECOND KORYPHAIOS

Yes, move along, but look sharp—that's what the lamps are for.
Watch out for pebbles—we can't have Jurors taking the rap!

SECOND LITTLE BOY

To the Second Koryphaios.

Daddy, Daddy, there's mud ahead—right there! Watch out!

SECOND KORYPHAIOS

Stopping and peering.

Dratted lamp—can't see. Take a twig and push up the wick.

SECOND LITTLE BOY

No, Daddy—I can push it up better with this. See?

He inserts his finger into the lamp.

SECOND KORYPHAIOS

Oh, you've got a head on *you*—waggle the wick with your finger—
and slosh all the oil—that expensive, hard-to-get-oil—

you IDIOT!
It's no skin off *your* nose when I have to pay those prices!

He hits the Second Little Boy.

There, that'll teach you!

SECOND LITTLE BOY

Any more lessons like that, Daddy,
and we'll blow out our lamps and go home. See how you like it alone—
you'll stumble and fumble and muck around like ducks in the dark.

SECOND KORYPHAIOS

I punish bigger and better men than you, sonny,
every. . . .

He slips.

Oops! the mud! I'm up to my knees in GUCK!
And look at all that snuff on the wicks—sure sign of a cloudburst
in three-four days. Oh, it's good for the crops—what's left of them.
Nothing like oceans of rain and a good, stiff, chilly North wind.

FIRST KORYPHAIOS

Well, here's Philokleon's house. Wonder what happened to him?
I don't see him waiting around to join the group. That's odd.
Never had to rout him out before. He was always first—
head of the line, singing the old songs. He's mad for music. . . .
That's an idea: we can . . .

*Suddenly to the Chorus, which is about to
plod right by.*

HALT!

The Chorus halts.

. . . *sing* him out to work.
—Places, men! Strike up a song; make it a good one!
Let's bring our crony out as fast as he can crawl!

FIRST SEMICHORUS

Singly.

Where's the old man? Why doesn't he come
to the door? Or at least say hello?
Do you suppose he lost his shoes?
That's sad. He could stub a toe.
Sprain an ankle. Strain a vein.
Rupture himself—you never know.

Tutti.

He's the nastiest man on the jury—
malign, marblehearted, and mean!
Though others may yield to defendants' appeals,
he thinks that acquittal's obscene!

SECOND SEMICHORUS

Singly.

What discomposed him? Yesterday's
false Friend of Democracy.
Our bogus Secret Agent in Samos?*
The defendant we let go FREE?
It infected our colleague. Fever. Colic.
Mercy is bad for his allergy.

Tutti, to the house.

Recover your health in the jury—
we're serving a traitor from Thrace.*
He's fat and he's flush and the pickings are plush!
Come down and we'll set you a place!

*A pause. Silence
from the house.*

FIRST KORYPHAIOS

All right, boy, let's move along.
*The First Little Boy steps to the center of the
stage, then stops.*

Come on, start up.

*The First Little Boy starts up, not the procession,
but a double duet with the Koryphaioi, molto con
espressione, in which the Boys parody the impossibly
pathetic youngsters whom Euripides would occasionally deprive of their mothers (as in the* Alcestis)
or feed to the Minotaur (as in the lost Theseus).

FIRST LITTLE BOY

O Father, gentle Father,
I beg of thee a boon.

FIRST KORYPHAIOS

Name me the toy; I'll buy it,
O best-belovèd Son.

FIRST LITTLE BOY

Not toys. I faint with famine;
a Fig to make me whole?

28

FIRST KORYPHAIOS

> A fig's too damned expensive,
> you glutton! Go to hell!

FIRST LITTLE BOY

> We'll refuse to light your way!

FIRST KORYPHAIOS

> I struggle every day,
> buying wood, and grain, and meat
> for the three of us to eat
> from my petty jury pay,
> you miserable pigs—
> Oh! Woe!
> > And you want Figs!

SECOND LITTLE BOY

> O Father dear, a query:
> Suppose they should decree
> *No Court Today*—where, Father,
> would that leave you and me?

SECOND KORYPHAIOS

> We wouldn't have the money
> to buy the food we want—
> before we could afford it,
> we could ford the Hellespont!

SECOND LITTLE BOY

> Poor Mother, why was I
> born into this world to di-
> et on wrangles and disputes,
> bitter writs and sour suits?
> Oh, the fruitless mimicry
> of my foodless little sack!
> Alas! Alas!
> > My life's a lack!

*The Little Boys dissolve into sobs, and the
Chorus seems about to follow suit. The threatened
inundation is staved off, however, by the appearance
of Philokleon at the window, behind the net. Quaver-
ingly he breaks into song, a song which bears a
rather horrid resemblance to the monody of a
shackled Euripidean heroine—Andromeda, say,
or Danae.*

PHILOKLEON

/ Aye weary do I waste at this aperture
lusting to list to your overture,
but heark for no hymns from me, Belovèd—
I cannot sing.
                    Whence, oh whence my deliverance?
They fence me pent 'neath dire surveillance
in durance vile, the while I burn,
yearning, to burst my bonds and sojourn
joined with you for some sweet spell . . .
in Court, and raise all kinds hell. /

The music changes.

O Zeus who launchest the lightning,
metamorphose me to smoke.
Infuse me with Proxenides' bluster,*
or the Flabber-Gas of Aeschines, son of Bloat,
and float me away on a tissue of lies.
Lord, shed sudden grace on Thy servant,
the slave of his convictions.
Cast on me a blast of unleavened levin,
roast me in the ash, catch me to heaven,
and waft me to rest in tartar-sauce . . .
or, better, Sovereign,
make me the rock on which they count
the verdict. Thanks. Amen.

FIRST SEMICHORUS

A point of information,
strictly *entre nous*—
Who shut you up? Who threw the bolt?
Who, dammit, who?

PHILOKLEON

It was my son—Phobokleon. But shhh! Don't shout—that's him
right there in front, asleep. So please, not so loud.

FIRST SEMICHORUS

What's behind this outrage?
Where do his motives lie?
We trust he adduced some flimsy excuse—
Why, dammit, why?

30

PHILOKLEON
He refuses to let me judge, or court any trouble. He claims
he intends to lap me in luxury at home. And I say no.

FIRST SEMICHORUS
That Fibberkleon's elusive!
Obviously evasive!
He means to muzzle a patriot
who dares expose the truth about
the way our Navy's going to pot.*
The evidence—conclusive:
your son's a SUBVERSIVE!

FIRST KORYPHAIOS
No time to waste. You need a novel synthesis, a striking
scheme to spring yourself without disturbing your offspring.

PHILOKLEON
Easy to say—but what? *You* try—I'm ready for anything.
I'm wild to stroll along the docket, just me and my ballot.

FIRST KORYPHAIOS
You require scope. Scoop out a hole somewhere and slip through,
muffled in rags, like Odysseus at Troy.

PHILOKLEON
Odysseus I tried
already. Not that hole. Besides, they've sealed the place—
no niche big enough for a gnat. Think of something else.

FIRST KORYPHAIOS
Remember our Navy days? When we took Naxos—and you took off
without leave? You stuck some stolen spits in the wall and *ran* down.

PHILOKLEON
Oh, I remember, but how does that help? I'm forty years older.
There's no resemblance.

THEN I was mighty—muscular—sly—
a matchless master at poaching.
All unperceived I could steal away . . .
besides, nobody was watching.
NOW I'm besieged by a whole damned army
loaded with ordnance, vigilant, vast.

31

Those two at the door are waiting to skewer me
like a common domestic pest.

AND the spits that I'd have to make do with
are the ones they'll run me through with!

SECOND SEMICHORUS
But now it's NOW, and it's morning!
This is an emergency!
Speed your planning! Improve the shining
hour, honey-bee!

PHILOKLEON
I'm afraid there's only one way open—to gnaw through the net.
—Pardon me, Artemis, goddess of traps! Don't be nettled.

SECOND SEMICHORUS
As Philokleon begins to chew the strands.
The man who squares his jaw is
the man who never succumbs.
Attack that mesh—forward, gnash!
Courage! Grind those gums!

PHILOKLEON
Well, it's done. I chewed it through.
The Chorus breaks into a cheer.
Stop that shouting!
Please proceed with caution—you'll wake up Phobokleon!

SECOND SEMICHORUS
Suspend your apprehension;
leave him to our discretion.
He'll cease his sacrilegious abuse
with his heart in his mouth!
With his heart in his shoes
he'll run for his life—and probably lose!
We'll stop his profanation
of Demeter's legislation!*

SECOND KORYPHAIOS
Now for a rope. Secure one end to the window, the other to you.
Then let yourself down. Slowly. Be brave; remember the motto:
Trust in Zeus, and take short views.

PHILOKLEON

Busy with the rope.

A teeny question:
If they should hook me on this line, and haul me back in—what then?

SECOND KORYPHAIOS

We'll call on our Courage, that old oaken Courage, and drive them
away!
They won't pen *you* up again—no, sir! We'll think of something.

PHILOKLEON

*Clambering into a rope seat and dangling just
below the window.*

All right. I place my life in your hands. If anything happens,
take me up, and mourn me, and bury me under the Bar.

SECOND KORYPHAIOS

Nothing is going to happen!

Of course, you might invoke
your ancestral gods before you slide. Why take chances?

PHILOKLEON

Dangling in prayer.

Lord of Lawsuits, Patron of Plaintiffs, Lykos my Master,*
whose eternal delights—even as mine—are the screams and wails
of convicted defendants; whose shrine is set,
the better to feast thine ears, at Court;
who choose, alone of the gods, to sit
on the losing side by the mourner's seat—
save thy neighbor, preserve him intact,
and nevermore, from this day hence,
will I piss on thy precinct or fart on thy fence.

*He descends slowly on the rope, as quietly as he
can. But his prayer has awakened Phobokleon.*

PHOBOKLEON

From the roof, to Sosias.

Hey, wake up!

Both slaves wake.

SOSIAS

What's wrong?

34

PHOBOKLEON

> A voice is whirring around,
I think. The old man didn't slip out another hole?

SOSIAS

Looking up.

> God, no! He's tied himself to a rope and sliding down!

PHOBOKLEON

Looking straight down and seeing his father.

> Again, you old cesspool? What do you think you're doing?
> Get back up there!

*Sosias pulls the blockade from the front door
and runs in. Xanthias, still fuddled, stands confused
until Phobokleon addresses him.*

> —Don't just stand there—
>
> climb up outside
> and hit him with the wreath!

XANTHIAS

> What wreath?

PHOBOKLEON

> The Thanksgiving wreath—
> over the front door, stupid! If we deck his bow, maybe
> he'll back his stern inside. But whatever you do, do it FAST!

*He disappears into the house. Xanthias grabs the
wreath from over the door and clambers up
the net, hand over hand. When he comes even
with Philokleon, he flails at him with the wreath.
During the next speech, Sosias and Phobokleon
appear at the window and haul the rope in slowly,
and Xanthias keeps pace with the rising Philokleon,
beating away.*

PHILOKLEON

Sorely beset, to the audience.

> A word to all this year's prospective plaintiffs—
>
> HALP!
> Hey, informers—Jekyll! Leech! You, Finque!
> And all you parasites—Skimpole! Grafton!
> Come on, fellows, you need me! Don't let them haul me back!

A little aid?

A little succor?

Last Chance—

*Just as Phobokleon and Sosias pull him through
the window.*

HAAALP!

*Xanthias follows him in, still flailing, and the four
disappear inside the house. The Chorus bursts
into action.*

FIRST KORYPHAIOS

Throwing off his cloak.

The Wasps are ruffled! Our nest's been disturbed! No Delay!
Let's churn up our Double-Distilled, Triple-Action ANGER!

*The members of the Chorus throw off their cloaks,
exposing their stings, which they raise to the ready.
The Little Boys collect the cloaks.*

ENTIRE CHORUS

Raise the Sting and hold it high, Boys!*
Show them how we stand,
fierce to cut and thrust for Justice,
feared throughout the land!

FIRST KORYPHAIOS

To the Little Boys.

Drop those cloaks! Run and shout the news to Kleon!

The Little Boys drop the cloaks and exit at a run.

ENTIRE CHORUS

Fight and smite the foe of Athens!
Hit with all your hate!
Show your Fury! Save the Jury—
Bulwark of the State!

A locomotive cheer:

AËRATE HIM!
PERFORATE HIM!
THAT'S THE WAY TO WIN!
OPEN UP HIS HEART AND LET THE
SUN
SHINE
IN!

36

Phobokleon emerges from the house, followed by
Xanthias, Sosias, and, in the clutches of the two
slaves, Philokleon.

PHOBOKLEON
Gentlemen, gentlemen, please! Stop shouting and hear my case.

FIRST KORYPHAIOS
We'll shout if we want to! As loud as we want to!
                                                    —Won't we, men?

PHOBOKLEON
It won't make a bit of difference. I refuse to let him go.

FIRST KORYPHAIOS
What's that? You WON'T? You refuse to obey the Voice of the
    People?

PHOBOKLEON
Precisely.

FIRST KORYPHAIOS
                Patent, plain, and obvious DICTATORSHIP!
To the audience.
            O Athens, Pearl of Attica!
                                    O Theoros, Peer of Debasement!
            O all you spongers,
                        scroungers,
                                    moochers,
                                            chiselers,
                                                    fatcats—
            in short, Everybody in Charge—
                                    DID YOU HEAR WHAT HE SAID?

SOSIAS
Holy Herakles, they DO have stings! Don't you see them, Boss?

PHOBOKLEON
That's what finished Philippos, the sophist—they ran him through
three suits in one afternoon. Completely gouged. Sad case.

FIRST KORYPHAIOS
And that's the way we'll finish YOU off!

37

To the Chorus, who complies with his orders.

COMPANY, TEN-*SHUN!*

RIGHT—*FACE!*

CLOSE—*RANKS!*

DRESS UP THAT LINE!

All right, men, let's put some spleen into it. Be Nasty!

Pointing at Phobokleon.

There's our objective! Make sure that he knows, in future, what sort
of a swarm he roused!

PRESENT . . . *STINGS!*

*The Stings, which have been sagging slightly, are
snapped to the ready again.*

READY, AIM. . . .

SOSIAS

God, this is awful—we're really going to FIGHT? *THEM?*
It scares me green just to see those prongs!

FIRST KORYPHAIOS

To Sosias.

Release that man!

I warn you, the time will come when you'll envy turtles their shells!

*He waggles his Sting wickedly. Sosias tries to bolt,
but is cuffed by Phobokleon, and continues, reluctantly, to hold Philokleon.*

PHILOKLEON

Colleagues! Jurors! Talesmen! Angry Wasps!

COME ON!

To the First Semichorus.

Mount a savage sortie there and spear them in the rear!

To the Second Semichorus.

A frontal attack—lance their fingers! Stab their eyes!

*Phobokleon leaves Philokleon with the slaves,
runs to the front door, opens it, and yells inside.*

PHOBOKLEON

Hey, Midas! Phrygian! Help—come here! You, too, Greedy!

*The three slaves trundle forth. Phobokleon
points at Philokleon.*

Grab that man! And don't let go of him for anybody—
because if you do, it's solitary confinement! Bread and water!

To the Chorus, as the three slaves fill in around
Xanthias and Sosias.

        Keep up your blather—I know what it means. Look at my father!
He hurries into the house. The First Koryphaios
continues to work on Sosias.

FIRST KORYPHAIOS
Let him go—unless you relish the prospect of being a scabbard!

SOSIAS
A *s-scabbard?*

FIRST KORYPHAIOS
      Or maybe a quiver.

SOSIAS

                A-quiver? God, I AM!
He attempts to bolt again, but is prevented by
Xanthias and the other slaves. Philokleon tries
another prayer.

PHILOKLEON
O Twi-formed Kekrops, Founder of Athens, hero-headed,
snake-shanked—Juror above, defendant below—
are you going to let an Old Athenian like me be mauled
by these FOREIGNERS? My foreigners? The ones I whipped
and whopped and taught to weep five quarts to the gallon—

                                 HUH?

SECOND KORYPHAIOS
The proof is plain—old age is nothing but a skein of agony.
What miserable evidence—two slaves mauling their poor old master!
Have they forgotten the love he covered them with in the old days?
The sheepskin jackets? The lambskin vests? The dogskin caps?
The care he showered on their feet each winter? No, their feet
didn't freeze; their hearts did. Look in their eyes: no gratitude,
no respect for anything old—not even old shoes.

PHILOKLEON
To Sosias.

Hear that? I'm kind, I'm considerate—

                    NOW will you let me go,
you dirty sonofabitch? Don't you remember all those skins?

Or yours—when I caught you stealing grapes, and took you out
to the olive-tree, and flayed you like a Man—forgot that?
I took the hide off clean—slaveskin all over the place.
You were *famous*—the Talk of the Town for weeks! But gratitude?
    Respect?
Not YOU!
With a nervous glance at the door.
                    Hurry up! He'll be back in a minute—LET ME GO!
Only Sosias is tempted, and the old man struggles
fruitlessly. The Chorus advances slowly toward
the slaves, who retreat, dragging
Philokleon with them.

FIRST KORYPHAIOS
To Xanthias and Sosias, who are in the fore-
front of the group.
          You can't delay your day of reckoning much longer, you two!
Then you'll know what manner of men WE are! Our hearts
are written on our faces—full of gall, and spleen, and law!
The Chorus presses on. The slaves and Philokleon
back toward the front door. Just as they reach it,
the door bursts open and Phobokleon bursts out,
carrying a club and a lighted torch. He gives
the club to Xanthias.

PHOBOKLEON
Hit them, Xanthias! Beat the Wasps away from the house!

XANTHIAS
I am, I AM!

PHOBOKLEON
Shoving the torch into Sosias' reluctant hands.
                   Smudge them out, Sosias! Smoke them off!

XANTHIAS
Swinging his club.
    GIT! GO TO HELL!

PHOBOKLEON
Pushing Sosias.
                 SCAT! GET OUT OF HERE!

SOSIAS
Eyes closed, torch held stiffly before him.
                              Shoo—please?

PHOBOKLEON
That's it, Xanthias! Club them, boy!

To the nearly catatonic Sosias.

—Pour on the smoke!

*The Wasps, merely very old men, are easily routed
and retreat without much resistance to the side of
the stage. The attack ceases. Phobokleon releases
Sosias, who opens his eyes, takes in the situation,
and swaggers over to the Chorus.*

SOSIAS
Scared off, huh? Could have told you—you didn't have a chance.

*The First Koryphaios brandishes his sting. Sosias
races back to his own group.*

PHOBOKLEON
Even *you* couldn't have driven them off so easily, Sosias,
if they'd been trained on different songs. Take the awful stuff
that Philokles writes. Why, they could strangle you with a single chord.

ENTIRE CHORUS

*To the same tune as the fight song, but
without the final locomotive.*

Now the Poor can see their Peril,
feel its slippery grip,
know its stealthy aggrandizement:
DREAD DICTATORSHIP!

SECOND KORYPHAIOS

Pointing at Phobokleon.

There's Exhibit A: the arrogant Autocrat himself!

ENTIRE CHORUS
See him keep us from our City's
Laws so flagrantly!
No excuses can confuse us.
He wants TYRANNY!

PHOBOKLEON

To the Chorus.

Is there any way to stop these fights, and that awful screeching?
Can't we hold a parley and come to some compromise?

SECOND KORYPHAIOS
Parley? Compromise? With YOU—an Enemy of the People?

Just look at you: the Compleat Pro-Spartan Aristocrat.
Those crazy tassels on your clothes spell Lunatic Fringe. And that
    messy
beard declares you're a hero-worshipping mimic of Brasidas.*
Parley with a Spartan-lover? To put it Laconically,

                                                  NO!

PHOBOKLEON

I'm tempted to let Father go. I can't fight a war every morning.

SECOND KORYPHAIOS

You think you have troubles now? This is just the appetizers! (Please
excuse our table-talk.) You don't hurt at all—not yet.
Just wait for the main course, down in Court, when the Public Counsel
carves you to bits with these charges. *Plus* a new one:

                                          SUBVERSIVE!*

PHOBOKLEON

Will you kindly get the hell out of here? Or is there a law
that says we have to stand here trading blows all day?

SECOND KORYPHAIOS

Leave? Desert my duty? Not while I'm alive! Me leave
a man unguarded who wants to bring DICTATORSHIP back?

PHOBOKLEON

"Dictatorship" and "Subversive"—that covers every case
you judge, large or small. Everything you do, in fact:
the universe in two nouns. It's the same way all over town.
I hadn't heard the *word* "Dictator" for fifty years
in Athens, and suddenly it's cheaper than smelt. It clutters up
the Market-place, chokes the shops—you trip on it.
Example. You don't want sardines for supper; what you want
is a nice, fat, juicy sea-bass. So down to the Mart you go,
and BUY a nice, fat, juicy sea-bass. And the man next door,
—who, incidentally, just happens to sell sardines—starts up:
"Sea-bass, huh? That's real rich food—expensive, too.
TOO expensive for a real Athenian democrat. Hey, Mac—
why the bass? You want to bring DICTATORSHIP back?"
Or say you're having herring for lunch, and you want an onion,
a pretty, round onion, to keep it company. Have you ever
tried to buy that onion? You do, and the woman next door—
you know, the one who sells scallions—takes a squint, and:

                                                                43

that Athens pays taxes so you can have fancy food? Hey, Mac—
why the onion? You want to bring DICTATORSHIP back?"

SOSIAS

Boy, are you right—you can't even get out of line in a whorehouse!
Yesterday noon I told this girl to climb on top
and you'd think I'd tried to start a revolution!
                                        "SUBVERSIVE!
There's only one way to do this," she says, "and that's flat!
You're trying to raise up Hippias' DICTATORSHIP!"
                                        I ask you!

PHOBOKLEON

I know. That's what goes in Court. It's music to *them*.
Take my case. All I want to do is keep Father away
from this early-to-Court-and-early-to-lie-and-do-the-defendant-
one-in-the-eye mode of existence; I want him to lead
a pleasant, luxurious, gentleman's life, like Morychos.
And what do they charge me with? Committing some heinous crime:
I'm a SUBVERSIVE; I'm plotting to restore DICTATORSHIP.

PHILOKLEON

By god, they're right, too! Can't you understand me, Son?
I don't WANT all this pie in the sky and pigeon's milk,
not me, not if I have to be barred, debarred, and disbarred
from the only life I know. And live like Morychos—why?
I'm not one of your goormays; I don't like eels, or rayfish.
What *I* like's a little lawsuit, chopped up fine
and stewed in its own juice. We call it a case-erole.

PHOBOKLEON

Habit, Father, sheer habit. A conditioned obsession—a deep one.
And yet, if you'll just keep quiet and listen to what I say,
I think that I can change your mind. I'll demonstrate
that your entire way of life is a Grand Mistake.

PHILOKLEON
I'm mistaken to JUDGE?

PHOBOKLEON

                    Worse. You're a butt, a laughingstock,
all unconscious, to men you nearly enshrine. In a word,
you're a SLAVE, and don't know it.

44

PHILOKLEON

Don't talk any slavery to ME—
I rule the WORLD!

PHOBOKLEON

Correction: you serve. Your rule's an illusion.
—All right, prove me wrong.
You "reap the fruits of Hellas"—
Demonstrate. Show us a fruit or two. Produce your profit.

PHILOKLEON
Will I ever!
Pointing to the Chorus.
I'll make a speech and let them arbitrate.

PHOBOKLEON
And so will I.
To the slaves.
All right, everyone, let him go.
The slaves obey and enter the house. Philokleon,
free, yells after them.

PHILOKLEON
And bring me a sword!
To Phobokleon.
By god, if I lose a debate with YOU,
I'll stick a sword in the ground, point up, and fall on it,
face down, the way Ajax did when he lost to Odysseus.
Sosias returns with a sword, gives it to
Phobokleon, and re-enters the house.

PHOBOKLEON
Handing the sword to Philokleon.

Pardon me,
but there's one little thing—the Oath.

PHILOKLEON

What Oath?

PHOBOKLEON

You should know more
about it than I do. The Oath where you specify the penalty you'll pay
if you fail to abide by the—how do you say it?—the disposition
of this debate.

PHILOKLEON

Oh, *that* Oath.

Sonorously.

I pledge myself to abide
by the just, impartial decision of this just, impartial Board
of Arbitration. If I should fail to do so, this be my punishment:
May I never, whenever the toasts go round, touch a drop—of my pay.

ENTIRE CHORUS

Arranged in judging position, it sings to Philokleon.

Defend the Old School's Honor!
Let none her Glory dim!
Be fresh in word and manner . . .

PHOBOKLEON

Breaking in on the Chorus, which holds on grimly
to the "-er," he calls toward the house.

Bring me out a tablet and a stylus—and be quick about it!

Noticing the Chorus' held note.

A fine exhibition he'll make, with a song like *that* to inspire him.

ENTIRE CHORUS

Continuing the song, with a baleful wave at
Phobokleon.

. . . but don't be fresh like *him!*
The verdict on your Great Debate
can overrule and abrogate
our Way of Life! The stakes are great.
If you incur the loss—
he's Boss!

PHOBOKLEON

Seated at a table, he receives the tablet and
stylus from Xanthias.

That's fine. He'll talk at random; I'll write at memorandum.

PHILOKLEON

Nervously, to the Chorus.

You were saying—what happens to us if he wins the debate?

ENTIRE CHORUS

We'll be reviled and called effete!
We'll be repealed as obsolete!
They'll only use us to complete
the files in some parade—
unpaid!

46

To Philokleon.

> And so, old friend, you who intend to debate and defend,
> from stern to stem, the range of our rule, the utter extent
> of our kingdom—courage! Extend your tongue to its utmost—
>
> > and utter!

PHILOKLEON

> I spring from the post to establish our claim as Best of Breed.
> No Crowned or Sceptred Potentate can surpass our power.
>
> > We're kings.
>
> The proof is plain: what creature on earth can match the delight,
> the luxury, power, respect, and glory that falls to the lot
> of that little old man, the simple Athenian Juror?
>
> > None!
>
> Example. I rise from my bed in the morning to find them waiting,
> the Men of Importance and Size (some of them *six feet tall!*),
> waiting for me, by the Bench. No sooner do I go inside
> than a tender hand steals into mine, still warm from tapping
> the Treasury. And then they beg, and bow, and wheedle, and whine.
> "Father," they say (they call me Father), "pity me, Father.
> You must have been a Quartermaster, or held a Public Trust.
> You know what it is to feather your nest. Pity me, Father."
> Do you think that a Very Important Person like that would know
> that I was alive, if I hadn't acquitted him once before?

PHOBOKLEON

> Yes, I'd better put that down. Let's see—
>
> > *Beggars.*

He writes the one word. Philokleon glares at him.

PHILOKLEON

> Well, sir, I'm all begged up, my bad temper's wiped off clean;
> I've made my promises of mercy—so I take my seat and proceed
> to forget every one. It's not that I shut my ears to the pleas;
> I listen to them all. Every rhetorical trick in the book
> is unfolded, and, as for kinds of flattery—well, if I haven't
> heard it in Court, it doesn't exist.
>
> > I'll be specific:
>
> First, The Paupers. They plead—or scream—that they're poor, and so
> Not Guilty. They heap their disasters so deep I almost believe them—
> they sound as poor as I am.

Next the Story-Tellers, with Fairy-Tales,
or little quips from Aesop, or else, on occasion, a Joke.
If I shake with laughter, the theory runs, I'll shed my anger.
I don't.

When this fails, and we sit like rocks, they summon The Kids
(as they're called)—the little girls and boys, dragged up by the hand.
They bend them down and make them bleat—and me, I listen.
Then the father, trembling with grief or fear (or maybe religion)
entreats me, as though he were praying to a god, to spare his
    children—
by acquitting *him* on the charge of embezzling public funds.
"If you delight to hear the bleat of a poor little lamb,"
says he, "be moved by the plea of this little lost sheep—my son."
Of course, if our taste is for pig-meat, he begs us to pity his daughter.*
(And in this case, I admit, we unscrewed our anger a bit.)
Well, now, I ask you: doesn't this show our position, and power—
a contempt for wealth which makes mere money something to laugh
    at?

PHOBOKLEON

I'll get that down. Point Two: *The money is something to laugh at.*
—But as Ruler of Hellas (you said it, I didn't), just how do you
    profit?

PHILOKLEON

How? Why, son, we have Sex, the Drama, Music, Money . . .
You name it!

First, we're the body that examines prospective citizens,
puts handsome boys to a probing to see just how they'll fit in
to the life of the City. We're thorough.

Or the Arts: Suppose an actor—
say Oiagros—is accused. He knows his plea had better consist
of that beautiful soliloquy from the *Niobe,* recited for us alone;
unless he'd rather be convicted.

And Music? Ever see a flute-player
when he's won a case? Notice sometime. He waits around,
reed at the ready, till Court's adjourned, to pipe a march
when the Jury retires.

Next, Money: A man dies with only a daughter,
but designates a son-in-law and heir in his will, all signed and sealed.

What do we do in Probate? We break that will to bits,
and assign those bits, *and* the daughter, to the highest . . . well,
  beseecher.
It's safe and easy, since nobody audits *our* books—No Other
Public Office Can Make That Statement.

PHOBOKLEON

                              True. Congratulations—
on *that* alone. But the poor heiress! That's downright immoral—
breaking a young girl's will and tampering with her entailment.

PHILOKLEON

But better is Respect: When the Senate and Assembly have trouble
  impeaching,
they pass a decree and remand the rascals to us for trial.
And then it's Pure Pie—Praise from the Greats of Athenian politics—
that clever young lawyer Euathlos, or maybe the famous athlete
(he holds the record for the shield-put) Flee-onymos.* They cover
  us with Love,
and say they'll "Uphold the Humble" and "Sweat for the Salt of the
  Earth."
What's more, no speaker can *ever* ram a motion through Assembly
without *our* votes. So Court adjourns early—short day, full pay.
Why, even *Kleon* respects us. He barks and flattens the rest,
but doesn't even snap at our heels. He's Our Defender, in fact:
He throws his arms around us and shoos the flies away—

Violently to Phobokleon.

                    a damned sight more than you ever did for your own father!
Or take Theoros. He's *Important* . . .

                              You know Theoros?

*A negative silence from Phobokleon.**

                    Why, everyone knows Theoros! *He's* like Euphemios—
that *Big!*

                    You *do* know Euphemios?

Another negative silence.

                              Well, take Theoros—
Know what he does? He takes a sponge and shines our shoes!
A man like that! Yes, sir!

                              Well, take a good long look.
Those are the profits you pen me away from. Count those Blessings;
then figure out how to convince me that I'm a SLAVE or a
  SERVANT!

Aside.

Talk till you're sick—and you will be. I'll show you up, soon enough.
You and your Holy Assizes! Ass-holes of Athens, that's you.
And your mighty Orbit of Influence—the ring you leave in the
    bathtub.

PHILOKLEON

But I almost completely forgot my greatest joy as a Juror:
I get my pay and go home at night, and they all see me coming,
and give me a big hello—just because of that money. My daughter
washes me off, and massages my feet, and calls me "Popsy,"
bends down for a kiss—and fishes the money right out of my mouth.
And the little woman talks sweetly for once, and serves me cake,
that puffy sweet cake, and sits beside me. "Go on and eat,"
she says, "there's more—eat it all." Then my star's at its brightest.
I don't have to worry about supper, and keep looking over at you
and that grumbling, grousing steward, who lives in terror that he might
have to make me another cake.

                    I have no worries *at all,*
thanks to my Bulwark, my Armor against the Slings and Arrows
and so forth. Refuse me a drink if you choose, I always have with me
my faithful donkey full of wine—

He drags from the folds of his cloak an enormous
wine-jar with two huge handles.

                     and I pour him myself.
And he opens his jaws, and brays at your bowls—

He drinks deeply from the jar, which gurgles
loudly, then sets it down.

                        and   farts   like   an
    army!
This is my job, my Empire—the Greatest Empire on earth!

He takes another drink.

    On earth?—

        Why isn't my Empire just as good as Zeus's?

        What they say about Zeus,
           they say about Me!
        When we kick up a fuss
           in fixing a fee,
      the passers-by rush
           and shout out, "Hey!
           Thunder in the Jury—
           Zeus Almighty!"

Faster yet; almost swelling into a god.
>   When I brandish the lightning
>   and throw it,
>   the rich men are frightened,
>   and show it—
>   they blubber! They shit, and
>   don't know it!
>   *And they're so mighty,*
>   *so hoity-toity!*

Assuming a statuesque pose, pointing an imperious
finger at Phobokleon, and going as fast as he can.
>   What's more, YOU'RE *scared*—
>   you, too!
>   YOU fear me! By GOD
>   you DO!
>   But I'M not afraid
>   of YOU!

Completely overcome by his divine role.
>   Puny, petty
>   *MORTALITY!*

ENTIRE CHORUS
>   A more persuasive lecture
>   these ears have never heard.
>   Such clarity! Such structure! . . .

PHILOKLEON
Relaxing into a strut, he interrupts the Chorus.
>   Yup. He must have thought he'd clip my vines by default;
>   he certainly knows well enough that *I* don't lose debates.

ENTIRE CHORUS
>   . . . Such Wizardry of the Word!
>   His speech sustained my self-esteem
>   and summoned me, in dream, to seem
>   Grand Juror in the Court Supreme,
>   to hear the Happy Isles'
>   retrials!

Phobokleon rises.

PHILOKLEON
Look at him shift his ground and fidget—no self-control!
—Before tonight, I'll make you look like a flogged dog, boy!

ENTIRE CHORUS

To Phobokleon.

No vain Chicane, no sly Finesse
can shake the Faith that I profess!
I only guarantee success
    to one Device, i.e.—
       be ME!

SECOND KORYPHAIOS

Wherefore, unless you really have something to say, my advice
to you is this: It's time to look around for a millstone,
sharp, fresh-hewn. Perhaps *it* can crush the edge of my temper.

PHOBOKLEON

Taking his place and addressing the Chorus.

To cure a disease so long engrained in the Body Politic
demands far more than the rude and feeble wit of a mere
Comic Poet. I begin, therefore, with a prayer from Homer:
Scion of Kronos, Zeus our father . . .

PHILOKLEON

                      Don't "father" me!
You show me how I'm a SLAVE, right quick, or I'll murder you!
God, what a thought! Murderers don't get fed at the Feasts!

PHOBOKLEON

Very well, *Daddy,* smooth your brow a little and listen.
First, some simple arithmetic.—No, not with pebbles;
use your fingers.
            Figure up the total of all the tribute
that Athens receives from the Federated States, and add to this
the direct taxes *plus* all those little one-per-cents,
court-costs, confiscations, mine-franchises, rents,
sales-tax, licenses, duties, tariffs, wharfage *and* tonnage,
and we get a sum of . . . roughly, twenty thousand talents.
Now deduct from this the annual pay of all the Jurors,
six thousand of you—at least, that's all we have for the moment—
giving us a total salary (let's see: six thousand Jurors,
three obols a day, eighteen days a month, times ten,
divide by six, divide by a hundred, divide by sixty)—
yearly, the Jurors cost Athens one hundred and fifty talents.

PHILOKLEON

Out of twenty thousand? We don't even get *ten per cent?*

PHOBOKLEON

Why, no. Not at all.

PHILOKLEON

But where does the rest of the money go?

PHOBOKLEON

Where? To the men with the mottoes, who will always "Uphold the
    Herd"
and "Sweat for the Salt of the Earth." So now you're held up and
    sweated,
and it's all your doing. *You* let them slather you in slogans, and *you*
elected them. To rule, of course, *you*. But not only you:
They petrify the Federated States with other slogans—e.g.,
"PAY THE TRIBUTE OR I ROLL THE THUNDER AND
    COLLAPSE THE CITY!"—
and proceed to squeeze fat bribes (fifty talents at a crash) for
    themselves;
while you, you're content to nibble the edges of your Empire's
    garbage.
The impression this makes on our Allies is not too hard to imagine.
They see you, the scum of Athens, weazening away on a diet
of ballot-box scraps, topped off, for dessert, with a succulent nothing,
and conclude, quite naturally, that you're as important as a fiddler's
    franchise.
So, without more ado, they turn to your leaders—and the stream
    begins.
They literally lave them in luxury: pillows, and dishes of fish,
honey, sesame, flagons of wine, firkins of cheeses,
cups and goblets, garlands and chaplets, clothing and carpets,
Health, Wealth, Long Life, Prosperity, and Such.
                                        While you—
the Ruler, the Founder, the Grand Panjandrum who shaped this
    Empire
with the strokes of your oar, on Land and Sea—from your vast
    domain
you derive not even one head of garlic to season your smelts!

PHILOKLEON

Well, that's true enough. I had to send out to a friend for three cloves
last night . . . but *this* is SLAVERY? Get to the point—you're
    killing me!

54

PHOBOKLEON

I submit this as Slavery in its most acute form: when men like those,
ringed by their toadies and jackals, can roll in public gold,
but you are, perforce, overjoyed if they dribble you three little obols!
What a fine reward for the toil and agony that won our wars!
Not precisely a reward, of course: you *work*. By the numbers, where
and when they tell you. And that's what sticks in my gorge,
when a fancy young pansy like Chaireas' brat (not even a citizen!)
waggles up to you, legs well apart, with that fairy air,
and orders you to be in Court early tomorrow:
$\qquad\qquad\qquad\qquad\qquad\qquad$ "If a *single* one
comes after they blow the signal, he simply *won't* get *paid!*"
But Time doesn't matter to *him;* he's a Public Prosecutor and draws,
come early, come late, *six* obols. Plus supplementary bribes from
$\qquad$ defendants.
These he splits with Defendant's Counsel—an intimate of his circle.
Then these strange bedfellows arrange the case, decide the outcome,
rough out a script, and fall to.
$\qquad\qquad\qquad\qquad\qquad$ You'd think they were handling a saw.
One pushes, one pulls—and, right in the middle, there's you.
$\qquad$ Watching.
For your pay, as it happens; so the whole sordid mess slips by you.

PHILOKLEON

That's what they do? To *me?* Do you mean it? Son, you're rocking
the bottom of my being—tugging at my reason—what ARE you
$\qquad$ doing?

PHOBOKLEON

Consider this rationally. You, and everyone else, could be *Rich*—
if you didn't let these Friends of the People keep you caged.
You *do* rule the world, or most of the world, from the Black Sea to
$\qquad$ Sardinia,
and what's your Profit?
$\qquad\qquad\qquad\qquad$ Your pitiful pay, doled out in dabs—
the exact amounts to keep you teetering on the edge of starvation.
They mean you to stay poor, don't you see? Their motive is obvious:
Hunger knows no friend but its Feeder.
$\qquad\qquad\qquad\qquad\qquad\qquad$ And so, whenever
your Tamers are threatened, they cluck their tongues, and flick your
$\qquad$ leash,
and you leap, ravening, on their enemies and tear them to bits.

But if these men *did* have the public welfare at heart,
it would be child's play to attain. Just take a look at the books:
At present, one thousand cities are paying tribute to Athens.*
Assign them each the board of only twenty Athenians—
and twenty thousand citizens would swim in savory stew,
and wreaths, and crowns, and cream, and Grade-A Milk and Honey,
tasting their fitting prize for saving Hellas at Marathon.
But, as things are now, you act like migrant olive-pickers:
no matter where he leads you, you follow the man with the obols.

PHILOKLEON

What's come over me *now?* I can feel my hand getting numb . . .
and the sword—can't hold it any longer. I'm soft as a grape.

PHOBOKLEON

Whenever you frighten your Masters, they say you can have Euboia,*
and fifty bushels of wheat apiece—
                               and you never get any.
No, I'm wrong: not too long ago, they gave you five bushels:
But you barely got *that,* of course—they accused you of being an
    alien—
they trickled it out by the quart—and it wasn't wheat—
                               it was barley.

Which is why I've kept you from the Courtroom premises.
You can't subsist on hollow promises,
on imitation ersatz substitutes,
steamed in scorn by chauvinist chefs.
You need Nourishment; I'm frantic to feed you;
Unlimited Menu—with a single proviso:
the larder and cellar are stuffed and unlatched,
so absolutely no more three-obol drafts
    of the Milk of the City Cashier.

SECOND KORYPHAIOS

Who said, *Don't judge till you've heard both sides*—remember? Re-
    gardless,
he had something there.
The Chorus huddles, then the First Koryphaios
turns to Phobokleon.

FIRST KORYPHAIOS

> This Body's thoroughly considered decision,
Sir, is that YOU WIN, by considerably more than a mile.
In token whereof, we unstring our rods of anger and office
and dip them to you.
> > —By the Numbers, Men: One, Two,
> > > DROOP!

The Stings, which have been at the ready, fall at
the command.

SECOND KORYPHAIOS

Now a word to you, dear friend of our youth, comrade in our creed:

SECOND SEMICHORUS

Picking up the cue and singing to Philokleon.

> Give in to his Logic, yield to his Proofs,
> > give in to his object—stop being obtuse!
> I wish *I* had a relative to tell me what to do
> so clearly and precisely, but the Lucky Man is YOU!

> > At your elbow there's a god;
> > > he's giving you a hand.
> > Take his favors. Don't be awed—
> > > accept them while you can!

PHOBOKLEON

> I promise all comforts prescribed for his years:
> gruel for his gums; chiffon; warm furs
> to keep out the cold; a whore to indulge
> in comprehensive below-the-belt massage.
> But look—not a word; not even a wheeze:
> I don't expect thanks, but I'm not exactly pleased.

FIRST SEMICHORUS

Singing to Phobokleon.

> He's come to his senses, returned to himself,
> > he's come to repentance—he's going to get well!
> He rues his rash litigiousness, his passion for so long.
> Be patient, please. He's just found out his every act was wrong!

> > For the future, you're his norm:
> > > he'll heed your eloquence;
> > he'll change his life, revise, reform—
> > > he *may* acquire some sense!

PHILOKLEON

OH, WOE, WOE, WOE, etcetera!

PHOBOKLEON

At last!—What's all the shouting for?

PHILOKLEON

In a Euripidean transport of grief.

Press not on me these paltry promises!
Lost are my loved ones! Reft am I left!
No more to tread those precious premises,
to hang on the Herald's accents soft:
"WE LACK ONE VOTE! WE'RE ONE VOTE SHORT!
WHO IS IT? DON'T NOBODY LEAVE THIS COURT!
STAND UP!"—and proudly to rise alone
and stride to the urns and cast the last stone!
—PRESS ON, O SOUL! ALL SPEED, O SOUL!
MAKE HASTE, O—
                    (Where'd I put that soul?)
—HITHER, SHADOWY ONE!
                              —And Kleon
better not let me catch him stealing
                    down in Court!
                    He better not!
                         He. . . .

The reversal is too much. He stands mute,
confused, bewildered.

PHOBOKLEON

Enough of this, Father. For heaven's sake, give in!

PHILOKLEON

I'll give in, boy. Anything you ask. Except—
don't ask me to renounce that *one* thing . . .

PHOBOKLEON

                              What one thing?

PHILOKLEON

My jury career. Before I give in on *that,*
they'll render the final verdict on me in Hades.

PHOBOKLEON

I know it's your greatest delight, and I won't stop you.
But don't go down to Court any more. What you need
is a change of venue. So stay right here, in the privacy
of your own home, and judge the servants.

PHILOKLEON

Judge the Servants,

boy? On what charge?

PHOBOKLEON

The charge doesn't change; just the Court.
For example, a simple misdemeanor: The maid "forgets"
to lock the door—she *says*. *We* prove Intent;
it's an open and shut case. So what do you do? You stick her—
with a smallish fine. One drachma. You've done it a thousand
times in Court. And this is Law at Leisure,
tailored to suit you, the easy, *rational* way.
If the day dawns bright, be a Solar Solon. Just move
the Court out into the sun. But suppose it snows.
Why freeze? There's Fireside Fining! Or, if it rains,
bring in your verdict—bring it inside, and be comfortable!
And sleep till noon, if you want; *then* open the session.
No official can turn you away for coming late
to your private jury box!

PHILOKLEON

Now, *that* sounds nice.

PHOBOKLEON

But that's not all—no, *Sir!*

Remember those endless
speeches when you were starving, eating your heart out
for a big, fat bite of Defendant, done to a turn?
Well, that's all over. Mix Litigation with your Lunch!

PHILOKLEON

Can I judge my best if I'm chomping on my food?

PHOBOKLEON

Better than your best! Your efficiency will double—triple!
It's a proven fact: in order to digest the evidence,
a jury needs to RUMINATE!

PHILOKLEON

You're getting there, Son.
I'm wavering. But there's one little point you haven't mentioned.
Who's going to pay me?

PHOBOKLEON

*I'*ll pay you.

PHILOKLEON

Well, that's just grand.
I'll draw all my pay to myself. Won't have to share it.
I've been burned on that.
                              The other day Lysistratos,
that practical joker, drew a drachma, the pay
for him and me, and got it changed at the fish-market.
Three obols for him, three for me. So I popped mine in
my mouth to take home, and—ugh! That taste! That smell!
I spat them out. He'd given me three mackerel scales!
That jokester! I started to haul him to Court, of course.

PHOBOKLEON

What was his reaction to that?

PHILOKLEON

Him? Oh, he said
that I had the belly of a billy-goat. "You're pretty quick
at digesting good, hard cash." That's what he said.

PHOBOKLEON

But no more of that for *you!* Another advantage
of the New Home Jury System!

PHILOKLEON

And no small one, either.

He ponders briefly.

Son, you've won your case; you can sign me up!
Let's get to the judging!

PHOBOKLEON

Wait right here. Don't move.
I'll bring out all the necessary equipment.

He enters the house.

PHILOKLEON

I can't believe my eyes. I heard a prophecy
once which said it was only a matter of time
before every Athenian judged cases right at home,
and built a little courthouse on his front porch,
right next to the shrine to Hekate. And it's coming true!

PHOBOKLEON

*Returning at the head of a column of slaves who
carry various improbable objects, he waves expan-
sively at them.*

And here we are. What do you say to *that?*
My original estimate has been greatly amplified.
For example, this.

He holds up an enormous jug.

PHILOKLEON

What's that?

PHOBOKLEON

A chamber pot.
Put the case that you're passing judgment and need
to pass water. This hangs right at hand. That prong
should hold it nicely.

PHILOKLEON

Son, that shows some sense!
And it's mighty thoughtful, too. Just the thing
for an old sea-dog like me. I'll have safe harbor
for a floating kidney.

PHOBOKLEON

Bringing a brazier and a bowl.

And here's a fire, and a bowl
of lentil soup. If you're hungry, warm it and eat.

PHILOKLEON

Now, that's ingenious! With colic or fever, I'll stay in,
and eat my soup, and still collect my fee!

Phobokleon advances with a rooster in a cage.

But why the rooster?

PHOBOKLEON

We provide for every contingency:
You know how defendants' speeches make you doze—
well, this cock crows you awake in time for conviction!

PHILOKLEON

All this is wonderful, son, but I miss one thing.

PHOBOKLEON

Name it.

PHILOKLEON

Do you think you could have them bring me
the shrine to the Juror's Protector—Lykos? I'd like it.

PHOBOKLEON

Caught flat-footed.

Why, certainly. It's—it's here already.

PHILOKLEON

Peering around.

Where?

PHOBOKLEON

*Desperate, then suddenly pointing at the huge
chamber pot.**

Here's the hero.

PHILOKLEON

That's Lykos?

PHOBOKLEON

Certainly.
You pour libations at a shrine, don't you? Well?

PHILOKLEON

Dubiously, to the chamber pot.

Master, please pardon me—but you were pretty hard
to recognize.

PHOBOKLEON

I don't see why. He seems as big
as Kleonymos.

PHILOKLEON

Looking inside the chamber pot.

You're right—another hollow hero.

PHOBOKLEON

The quicker you sit down, the quicker I'll call
the first case.

PHILOKLEON

Taking a seat.

Son, I was sitting before you were born.
Call away!

PHOBOKLEON

In a worried aside.

Let's see. What case to introduce first?
Just who in this house has done anything wrong?

Oh, well—

Raising his voice to an official bellow:

CALL THRATTA, THE MAID, FOR BURNING UP—

PHILOKLEON

Hold it, son!

You'll be the death of me! Imagine calling a case
in a Court without a Bar!

PHOBOKLEON

A Bar?

PHILOKLEON

That fence
between the jury and everyone else. Why, that's
the holiest thing in Court. You want bad luck?

PHOBOKLEON

We don't *have* a Bar.

PHILOKLEON

Well, I'll run inside and get one.
I can rustle one up right away—need a Bar. Watch!

He dashes into the house.

PHOBOKLEON
What next, I wonder? Habit's an awful thing.
Xanthias runs out of the house, yelling over his shoulder.

XANTHIAS
Go to hell!
Muttering.
Try to feed a dog like that!

PHOBOKLEON
What's the matter?

XANTHIAS
What else *could* be the matter?
That grabby dog Chowhound,* of course! Jumped into the pantry,
clamped onto a rich Sicilian cheese and gulped
the whole thing down!

PHOBOKLEON
That's *it!*

XANTHIAS
What's *what?*

PHOBOKLEON
The *crime*—
the first case I'll introduce to father for judgment.
You stay here and prosecute.

XANTHIAS
Not on your life,
not me!
But the other dog there says *he'll* prosecute,
if someone files a charge.

PHOBOKLEON
Excellent! Fine!
Go bring them both out here.

XANTHIAS
Just as you say, Sir.

He exits into the house. After a short pause,
Philokleon emerges from the house, carrying a
section of fence.

PHOBOKLEON
What in the world is *that?*

PHILOKLEON

The pigpen. Our Bar.

PHOBOKLEON
You mean the pen for the pigs we sacrifice to Hestia?

PHILOKLEON
Yup.

PHOBOKLEON
But that's sacrilege!

PHILOKLEON

Not sacrilege—sacri*fice.*
Lets the defendant know where he stands. Be fair,
that's what I say.

But bring on that first case—
I've got that old conviction-itch.

PHOBOKLEON

One moment.
We need the docket and the indictments.
He enters the house.

PHILOKLEON

I tell you, boy,
you're grinding me down. Delays, delays, delays—
you're killing me!
He shows the wax tablet he uses to pass sentence.
I only want to plow
a nice long furrow in my little field here.

PHOBOKLEON
Returning with some scrolls.
Here we are.

PHILOKLEON

Then call that first case!

PHOBOKLEON

Pretending to peruse the scrolls.

Let's see;

who's first . . .

PHILOKLEON

Tarnation!

PHOBOKLEON

What's wrong?

PHILOKLEON

I forgot the urns—

the Jury's ballot boxes! Makes me sick!

He rises.

PHOBOKLEON

Hey, there! Where are you going?

PHILOKLEON

To get the *urns!*

PHOBOKLEON

Sit down; I saw to that. We'll use these pots.

He places two small pots on the table.

PHILOKLEON

That's pretty—real pretty. We've got everything,
all we need. Except—

where's the water-clock?

*He rises. Phobokleon pushes him down and points
at the chamber pot again.*

PHOBOKLEON

There.

PHILOKLEON

That? A water-clock?

PHOBOKLEON

What else could it be?

PHILOKLEON

Dubiously.

Er—sure.

He shrugs and surveys the scene happily.

Well, nothing's missing. You know the Court like a native.

PHOBOKLEON

Calling into the house.

Bring out the myrtle, the incense, the holy fire!
And hurry! Court can't be convened before
we invoke the gods and beg them for their blessings.

Slaves from the house bring the desired articles.

FIRST KORYPHAIOS

To Philokleon and Phobokleon.

From war and trouble
you've made a noble
      metamorphosis.
And so, to your vows
we add our prayers
      for your success.

To the Chorus.

Now let holy silence
preface our petitions.

ENTIRE CHORUS

Pythian God
Apollo, heed
our hymn and bless our word.
Attune the plan
of this young man
to *our* existence, Lord.
And may it bring
our wandering
to rest in clear accord.
      Hail, Paian—Healer!

PHOBOKLEON

Mighty Apollo, God of the Ways, Watcher at the Gate,
receive this rite, newly minted, fresh for my father.
Soften and supple the stiff, the unbending oak in his soul;
honey and mellow his temper's tartness, the must of his heart.

Sweeten him, Lord, to the human race,
prone to pity, tending to tears,
tears for the suppliant,
tears for the victim—
none for the plaintiff—
his bitterness bottled,
his anger unnettled.

ENTIRE CHORUS

The canons you
set forth, so new,
provide for us a key.
Our descant prayers
we raise to yours
in perfect harmony.
This note of grace
from youth to age
is no set cadency.
Hail, Paian—Healer!

*The prayer over, the Chorus retires to the wings
and Xanthias brings from the house two dogs,
Chowhound (the defendant) and Fleahound (the
plaintiff). Phobokleon, who acts the parts of various
court officials during the succeeding scene, addresses
the Jury—Philokleon—now in the manner of
a herald.*

PHOBOKLEON

OYEZ! ALL JURORS IN THEIR SEATS! POSITIVELY NO
ADMITTANCE TO THE BOX AFTER THE COMMENCE-
MENT OF DEBATE!

PHILOKLEON
Settling himself.

Who's the defendant?

PHOBOKLEON
Pointing at Chowhound.

He is.

PHILOKLEON

Oh, what I've got
in store for him—Unanimous Conviction!

PHOBOKLEON
                              ATTENTION!
THE INDICTMENT: THE CASE OF FLEAHOUND, OF
    KYDATHENEA,
VS. CHOWHOUND, OF AIXONE! THE CHARGE: UNLAWFUL
POSSESSION AND SELFISH DESTRUCTION OF ONE
    SICILIAN
CHEESE! PROPOSED PENALTY: IMPOUNDMENT, THIRTY
LEASHES, AND PERMANENT CONFINEMENT IN A
    WOODEN COLLAR!

PHILOKLEON
A stock penalty. They're getting soft. When *I*
pass sentence on him, by god, he'll die like a dog!

PHOBOKLEON
THE DEFENDANT CHOWHOUND WILL ADVANCE TO THE
    BAR OF JUSTICE!

PHILOKLEON
As the terrified dog shambles up to the railing in
front of him.
                Criminal Type. I can spot them every time:
                Pointy ears, eyes set close together, weak chin,
                wet nose . . .
Chowhound gives a dog's yawn.
                              There! See that? He's showing his teeth!
                Trying to Intimidate the Jury, eh? I'll fix him!
                —But where's the plaintiff? Where's this Fleahound fellow?

FLEAHOUND
GRRRRROWF!

PHOBOKLEON
Weakly.

He's here. Another Chowhound, that's what he is.

PHILOKLEON
Now, wait. You must admit he's a powerful barker . . .

PHOBOKLEON
. . . and licker of pots. And boots.

71

PLAINTIFF, MOUNT THE STAND AND BRING YOUR CHARGE!

Fleahound mounts a bench. Philokleon turns to the
brazier where the soup is heating, and pours out
a bowlful.

PHILOKLEON

This seems a good time to sustain my judgment with soup.

FLEAHOUND

In a roar, the volume varying, seemingly at random,
from very loud to much louder.

Gentlemen of the JURY! You have already HEARD the writ
I WROTE, and there's no point in reading IT again!
That mealy-mouthed MONGREL there is ACCUSED
of High CRIMES and MISDEMEANORS—i.e., he cheated
ME! and all the yo-heave-HO boys in our NAVY!
Just what did this PUTRID pooch do? He BOLTED away
into a corner, a DARK corner! And there
he GUZZLED up a WHOLE CHEESE—
SICILICED it to bits!

PHILOKLEON

Yup. True enough. That stinker belched just now,
and I nearly got choked by the smell of cheese! GUILTY—
out of his own mouth.

FLEAHOUND

And *I* DIDN'T get a BITE!
Look here—WHO'S going to help you OUT—WHO'S
going to look AFTER you, if people start to STOP
kicking in—I MEAN, throwing a SCRAP
or two to ME, your faithful HOUND—Your BODYGUARD?

PHILOKLEON

Indignant.

And he didn't give any to *me,* the Body Politic!
Oh, but he's a sly one—sharp—he bites—
just like this—ouch!—soup. Dammit, it's hot!

PHOBOKLEON

Father, for heaven's sake! You can't condemn him
before you've heard both sides!

72

PHILOKLEON

                                               Oh, come, now—look

at the facts. The case is clear.

With a wave at Fleahound.

                                      It barks for itself.

FLEAHOUND

You CAN'T acquit him—of ALL the dogs in the WORLD,
that man's the SELFISHEST greedyguts there IS!
Know what he DID to that Sicilian HOARD?
He sailed AROUND the plate—

                            he STRIPPED the rind

off all the CHOICEST sections, and wolfed it DOWN!
All that was LEFT was the HOLES!

PHILOKLEON

Holding up a flap of his motheaten cloak.

                                    And I got those.

FLEAHOUND

One more REASON to PUNISH him . . .

PHOBOKLEON

                                  . . . is because

one trough isn't big enough to feed two thieves?

FLEAHOUND

. . . is THIS—to serve your FAITHFUL HOUND! Don't let
my BARKING go in vain! If he goes FREE,
I'LL NEVER BARK *AGAIN!*

PHILOKLEON

                              Bravo! Bravo!

Fleahound bows and steps down.

        Now *that's* an accusation—crimes and more crimes!

Pointing to Chowhound.

                                          That man's

solid larceny!

To the rooster.

                You agree, old cock?

                            By god,

he winked!

        —Bailiff! Where's the Bailiff?

PHOBOKLEON

I'm here.

PHILOKLEON

Well, pass me the pot!

PHOBOKLEON

Get it yourself. I'm also
Herald, and it's time for me to call the witnesses.

*Philokleon rises and avails himself of the
chamber pot.*

I CALL THE WITNESSES FOR THE DEFENDANT
CHOWHOUND.

*As he summons them, a host of kitchen implements
emerge from the house and take up positions
before him.*

BOWL!
GRINDER!
CHEESE-GRATER!
GRILL!
STEW-POT!

AND ALL THE OTHER UTENSILS UNDER SUBPOENA!
—Haven't you finished pissing yet?
BE SEATED!

PHILOKLEON

Don't need to, son—but I know someone who *will:*

He leers savagely at Chowhound, who cringes.

Oh, am I going to scare the shit out of him!

PHOBOKLEON

Don't be such a compulsive grouch. Whenever
you see a defendant, it's always dog-eat-dog.
—THE DEFENDANT WILL MOUNT THE STAND AND MAKE
HIS PLEA!

*Chowhound, in terror, climbs on the bench and
trembles, unable to utter a sound.*

Well, say something! Speak *up,* dog! Make your plea!

PHILOKLEON

I don't think there's a single thing he *can* say.

PHOBOKLEON

No, you're wrong. I know the trouble—he's sick.
I saw it happen to old Thoukydides once*
when he was on trial:
                        Litigation Lockjaw.
It comes on suddenly. No immediate cure.

To Chowhound.

All right, down, out of my way.
                        I'll defend you.

*Chowhound leaves the bench; Phobokleon mounts
it and addresses Philokleon.*

Gentlemen of the Jury:
                        Give a dog a bad name,
and his defense in a Court of Law becomes difficult.
But I shall make the attempt—make it because
he is A Good Dog, and chases away the wolves.

PHILOKLEON

He's a thief, too—and worse than that, a SUBVERSIVE!

PHOBOKLEON

I object. Of all today's dogs, this is Best in Show.
The perfect type to tend a huge and brainless
flock of sheep.

PHILOKLEON

                        What profit is that?—HE EATS
THE CHEESE!

PHOBOKLEON

                        What profit? List his points: he fights
your battles, guards your premises—what profit?

PHILOKLEON

                                                HE EATS

THE CHEESE!

PHOBOKLEON

                        Oh, yes, the cheese.
                                        So he steals a little—
and why? Because he's rough and tough—and that's
the thing we need, in a dog or a general.
                                        Pardon
his lack of polish; he never studied the harp.

PHILOKLEON

Holding up a scroll.

> I wish he'd never learned to write. Or hide things.
> He buried that cheese somewhere in his Statement to the Court.

PHOBOKLEON

Stepping down.

> Please try to be fair and hear my witness out.
> —CHEESE-GRATER, MOUNT THE STAND!
>> Now then, speak up.
> When Chowhound is alleged to have seized the Sicilian cheese,
> you held the post of steward?

The Cheese-Grater nods.

>> Now then, answer clearly:
> Did you portion out your receipts to these soldiers here?

*He gestures at the other utensils. The Cheese-Grater
nods. Phobokleon addresses Philokleon.*

> —He affirms that the soldiers received the regular grate.

PHILOKLEON

> I say he's lying—his story's full of holes!

PHOBOKLEON

> Oh, Sir, I implore your compassion. Pity the underprivileged.
> Behold the luckless Chowhound! His only sustenance
> the scrapings of tables, the heads of fish!

Chowhound fidgets madly.

>> Condemned
> to a restless existence—a rover with no place for his head!

With a wave at Fleahound.

> Compare this sleek, well-kenneled cur. What profit?
> *His* profit. A watchdog—an *inside* watchdog, who snarls
> for his cut when anyone enters. And gets it—or bites.

PHILOKLEON

> But what's bitten ME? I'm sick—I'm going all soft
> inside! I can feel it slithering, winding over me—
> the Juror's fatal disease—*Creeping Persuasion!*

PHOBOKLEON

> Gentlemen of the Jury, O Father, heed now my entreaty.
> Harden not your hearts, but melt it in mercy!*
> Deign not to demolish this dog!
>> —Where are the children?

*Xanthias herds a group of crying puppies out of
the house.*

MOUNT THE STAND, O POOR, O PITIFUL PUPS!

*The puppies climb the bench beside Phobokleon,
who cuddles them.*

You sorry, stricken whelps of a helpless hero,
Whine!
     Whimper!
          Weep!
              Beseech the Court
to melt in Simple Humanity for your miserable sire!

*The air is rent with hideous doggy howls. Philokleon
is reduced to tears.*

PHILOKLEON
Stop! I can't stand it! Step down! STEP DOWN!

PHOBOKLEON
                      I shall
step down, though I know that Jurors' Trap, that Quasi-Legal
Fiction. You let the defendant think he's won
by shouting "Step Down!" and down he steps, breaks off
his defense—whereupon you convict him. Nevertheless,
I shall step down . . .

PHILOKLEON
Recovering his spleen at the last moment.
            . . . STRAIGHT
                TO
                HELL!

Disgustedly throwing down his soup-bowl.
                  This eating—
It's no good, that's all. Just now I melted every grain
of Sense I own in tears—and why? Because
I was full of hot soup, that's why!

PHOBOKLEON
              You mean he's *convicted?*

PHILOKLEON
It's difficult to tell at this point. The votes aren't in.

PHOBOKLEON
Father, dear Father, turn to Finer Things!

To kindness, and justice! Take this pebble and close
your eyes for the painful task, the work of a moment.
Speed to the Second Urn and *acquit* him, Father!

PHILOKLEON

No, son, those Finer Things aren't for me. Pardon
my lack of polish; I never studied the harp.
He starts for the table with the voting urns.
Phobokleon intercepts him and grabs his arm.

PHOBOKLEON

I'll take you over, Father; I know a shortcut.
He leads Philokleon to the table by a route which
includes a number of dizzy twirls, so that when his
father arrives before the table, he is quite confused.

PHILOKLEON
Pointing to the Second Urn. The markers of the
Urns, if any, are turned away from him.
Is this the First Urn—the one for "GUILTY"?

PHOBOKLEON

That's it.

PHILOKLEON
Dropping his voting-pebble in the Second Urn.
Then there's my vote!

PHOBOKLEON
Aside.

He took the bait! In spite
of himself, he voted to acquit!
—I'll tally the votes.

PHILOKLEON
Impatiently.

Well, what's the verdict?

PHOBOKLEON

Time will tell. Be patient.
He empties out the Urns, one after the other,
very deliberately.
—THE DEFENDANT CHOWHOUND IS FOUND TO BE *NOT*
GUILTY!

Philokleon falls senseless to the ground.

Father, Father, what's wrong?

Oh, *dear!*

WATER!

*Xanthias dashes up with a jug of water and empties it
over Philokleon.*

Excelsior, Father!

PHILOKLEON

Struggling up feebly on one elbow.

Don't play tricks on me, Son.
Was he really, truly acquitted?

PHOBOKLEON

I swear it.

PHILOKLEON

Falling back.

I'm extinct.

PHOBOKLEON

Don't brood—put it out of your mind. Here now, stand up.

He helps Philokleon rise and supports him.

PHILOKLEON

But how can I live with what I've done? How
can I bear that dreadful load on my conscience? How?
I ACQUITTED A DEFENDANT! What evil fate will befall me?

Raising his arms to heaven.

O gods on high, adored and honored, absolve your
servant, a sinner in spite of himself! My nature
is not so heinous as to plot a deed like that!

PHOBOKLEON

Of course it isn't. Away with these worries, Father.
Place yourself in my hands. My sole concern
will be your care and comfort. The two of us
will go *everywhere* together, sampling all
the sophisticated, genteel joys that Athenian society
offers—dinners, banquets, parties, and the theater.
The balance of your days will pass in utter bliss,
and never again will you play the demagogues' dupe.
Let's go inside.

A broken man.

                    All right, Son, if you say so.
They enter the house, Philokleon guided tenderly
by his son, followed by the puppies, the utensils,
the dogs, and the slaves.

            FIRST KORYPHAIOS
                    Hail and farewell, friends!
                    May fortune attend your
                            every venture!
Turning to the audience.
                    Meanwhile, to you Numberless Millions,
                    I offer a message of caution:
                    PROTECT YOUR GOOD NAME.
                    The ensuing remarks contain
                    pith and profit in plenty;
                    and any self-respecting
                    audience, caring at all
                    to avoid the general
                    appellation of IGNORAMUS
                    —and worse—really must
                    be improved thereby.
                            Verbum sap., say I.
Stepping forward.
                People of Athens, prove your vaunted taste for Truth
                and attend the Complaint which the Poet brings against the spectators.
                WANTON INJURY, WITHOUT PROVOCATION, AGAINST A
                    BENEFACTOR—
                so runs the charge brought by Our Bard.
                                        He was ever your Savior,
                from his first, incognito essays at the stage—when he took a leaf
                from the book of that supple, sage ventriloquist-prophet EURYKLES,
                and cast his very self and voice into others' mouths*
                to pour forth a purest stream of comedy, funny and ribald—
                down to the day when he threw off the mask and ran his own risks,
                charioteer for his own, his private stable of Muses.
                Through all that time your safety and comfort was his only concern.
                And then, when you raised him, and prized and praised him as none
                    before him,
                did conceit inflate and balloon his brain? Perhaps he perverted
                his talents and titles, scouring the schools for talented perverts
                (like certain comedians who shall be nameless*)?

What's more, if a thwarted pederast pressed him to slander a boy-love
back into bed, he refused. His Muses are public servants,
not private pimps; his sense of fitness knows Right from Wrong.

—Next, his aims are high. When he took to the stage, he attacked no
  MEN,
but with Herakles' courage and rage he loaded his Chorus for
  MONSTER
and marched on the mighty, assailing all manner of Gogs, Magogs,
and Demagogues. From his first performance,* he dared to measure
  his strength
with that rankest of reptiles, the Brown-Tailed, Saw-Toothed
  KLEONOSAURUS REX.
Its eyes flashed fire with a whorehouse glare, while in its hair
in a writhing mass, a hundred heads of lousy leeches
circled and weaved—and kissed its foul ass. It screamed in the voice
of a roaring river in labor, and bore the stink of a seal,
the greasy balls of a female troll, the rump of a camel.
But before this sight, did our dauntless poet take fright—or a bribe?
No, friends, not a bit. For you he warred then—for you he wars now.

Again, last year he turned his sights on those vampire demons
of chills and fever who stole by night to strangle fathers
and suck the breath from fathers' fathers; who then lay down
in their beds to plot and paste together a cruel collage
of suit and summons, writ and witness, against the harmless.
He attacked these informers* with such success that many leaped,
scared out of their wits and beds, to complain to the courts that they,
as alien goblins, were suffering torture commonly reserved
for full-fledged citizens.
                    In short, you'd found a Champion to cleanse
and purge your city of evil—
                    Wherefore (and here's the core
of the Complaint) last year, when your Savior sowed New Ideas by
  the sackful,
your heads were so hard that you ruined his crop. Nothing came up.
You betrayed him, and gave, in your idiot folly, LAST PRIZE to
  THE CLOUDS!—
to the best of all comedies ever performed (a firmstanding fact,
which Our Author repeatedly urges the god Dionysos to witness).
This award confers dishonor on YOU, for slow-witted dullness.

ARISTOPHANES suffers no slur from those with a *right* to opinions:
he wrecked his hopes—
                         but only because he was passing his rivals.
                              Hence, for the future,
                              you witless wonders,
                              when poets you find
                              with freshness of mind
                              who exhibit intentions
                              toward novel invention
                              of thought or expression,
                              cherish them, nourish them,
                              cull their conceptions
                              and carefully place
                              them in chests with sachets—
                              and through the next year
                              the clothes that you wear
                              will give off an air
                              of ineluctable savior-faire.

        Long ago—
                    We were mighty in the dance,
                    we were mighty at advance,
        and our mightiness resided in the sting we bear;
                    but our power didn't last,
                    and our lustihood is past,
        and whiter than the swan fade the flowers of our hair.

                    From these remnants we must recover
                    some spark, some trace of youthful vigor.
                         And my old age
                         is more than a match
                         —at least, in my estimation—
                    for the pansy poses, girlish curls,
                    and happy homosexual whirls
                    of the younger de-generation!

And now, to you in the audience who swell with confusion, curiosity
pricked by these spiky stings, intellects squeezed by our wasp waists,
a palliative explanation: the cause of our costume in a very few words,
words carefully chosen so as not to puzzle the dullards among you.

We, then, whom you behold so sharply appointed, are *Attic*
(and thence contentious)—the only authentic race of Attica,
tracing our lineage to those sprung from the soil by spontaneous
   generation.
For virulent virility, we remain unmatched. At Pest Removal,
the City has not known our peer in sheer belligerence, as witness
the coming of the Persians.*
                           Their aim was simple—to drive us from
   our hives.
And they put the entire City to the torch to supply the smoke.
Straightway, forth we swarmed, our bravery bolstered with gall.
We took our stand with shield and spear in single combat,
and ground our jaws with ire as they blotted out the sun with arrows.
But the owl of omen flew over our ranks before the attack,
and when evening blotted the sun in truth, the Persians bolted,
routed. We raced behind and riddled their Oriental rears,
while their jaws and brows ballooned, harpooned by our Sting.
                                    Wherefore,
since men are known by their attributes, throughout barbarian lands
we are famed as the manliest race alive: the ATTIC WASP.

SECOND SEMICHORUS
    Then it was—
            I inspired so much dread
            that I never was afraid;
   when I sailed against the foe I made him kneel or flee;
            for my mind was free and clear
            of these new civilian fears:
  "Can I make a good rebuttal?"
                  "Who'll inform on me?"

     The only conviction that ever we bore
     assigned the verdict to the fastest oar.
         And that we plied;
        but now must plead
       Guilty in the First Degree
     to pillaging the Persians' power
     of gold, and thus providing for
     our young delinquents' larceny.

SECOND KORYPHAIOS
Observe us, and you will find complete correlation between
our habits, manners, ways of life, and those of Wasps.

Imprimis: The world holds no other creature which, when ruffled,
can hope to approach us in presence of rancor or absence of temper.
And all our other activities are equally nasty and waspish. //
Clumped together in swarms we sit in our *hives,* you might say—
the Archon's Court, the Eleven's Court, the converted Odeion*—
and render judgment.

                    We're packed in solidly, squeezed against
the walls, bent double right down to the ground, not able to move.
Compare the wasp-grubs, sealed in cells.
            //We're industrious, too.
To win subsistence by stinging *everyone* without distinction
is Very Hard Work—and that's the way we earn our living. //
There, too, comes trouble: we have our drones, who laze among us
but have no stings, and yet, in their pointless existence, devour
the fruit of our labors without a hint of motion or effort,
not even a bit of bitterness.
                  But our greatest vexation is to view
our salary swilled by a NON-VETERAN slacker, whose hand never
    knew
oar, nor lance, nor blister upraised in his Country's defense.
Hence, my decision:
                In future, no citizen without a sting
may draw the Juror's three obols. Briefly:
                      No prick, no pay.

*The Chorus retires. Philokleon stumps from the
house in vexation, clutching his threadbare cloak
with the tenacity of a drowning man. He is followed
by the equally tenacious Phobokleon, who carries a
new cloak of Persian make, very shaggy, which
he is intent upon exchanging for his father's old one.*

    PHILOKLEON
Pressing his cloak desperately to his bosom.
        If you take me out of this cloak, it'll be feet first!
        We were in the service together—it saved my life!
        There we were, shoulder to shoulder, standing off
        the first attack of the winter—I might have frozen!

    PHOBOKLEON
    I don't think you appreciate nice treatment, Father.

    PHILOKLEON
    Why should I? Just costs me money.

Take eating—
I filled up on herring yesterday, and so it cost me
three obols—a whole day's pay—to get *this* cloak cleaned!

PHOBOKLEON
I'm afraid you don't have much choice.
You know the agreement.
You've made me your legal guardian, once and for all.

PHILOKLEON
Sulkily.

Oh, all right. What do you want me to do?

PHOBOKLEON
Simple. Take off that worn, sleazy old cloak,
and put on this bright, spanking new robe here.
Be the smart, natty man of the world you really are,
*He removes the old cloak from his father, who,
though resigned, is none too co-operative. The
process is thus rendered rather more difficult than
it should be.*

PHILOKLEON
Emerging at length from his cloak.
What's the point in having children, anyway?
I fathered him, and now he smothers me.

PHOBOKLEON
Proffering the robe.
Less chatter and more action—put this on!

PHILOKLEON
Son, will you tell me what the hell this *is?*

PHOBOKLEON
It's Persian—they call it a burnoose.

PHILOKLEON
Burn whose?

PHOBOKLEON
Or else an astrakhan.

PHILOKLEON
I thought it was a scatter rug.

PHOBOKLEON

Understandable—you've never been to Sardis
on one of those embassies. If you had, you'd know
what it is.

But now you don't.

PHILOKLEON

You're right enough there—
It looks to me like Morychos' overcoat—

with Morychos

still inside it.

PHOBOKLEON

It's *Persian,* I tell you—woven
in Ekbatan. It's an *astrakhan!*

PHILOKLEON

ASS-trakhan?
Those tricky Persians'll fleece anything that walks.

PHOBOKLEON

Oh, stop it, father. This is a Persian burnoose,
woven in Ekbatan at absolutely ruinous expense.
One of these consumes sixty pounds of wool.

PHILOKLEON

Hungriest looking cloak I ever saw.

PHOBOKLEON

PLEASE STAND STILL AND PUT THIS ON!

PHILOKLEON

Accepting reluctantly and sniffing.

Pew!—

You're right, it's astrakhan.
He starts to slip it on.

Burnoose, too—

God, it's hot in there!
He takes it off.

PHOBOKLEON

PUT THAT THING ON!

PHILOKLEON
I won't. Son, if you feel like this, why not
stick me in the oven right away? It's quicker.

PHOBOKLEON
Very well, *I'll* put it on you.
He envelops Philokleon in the shaggy robe, then
notices the old cloak lying on the ground. All his
frustration emerges in a violent kick at it, ac-
companied by an address.
                                        Get out of here!

PHILOKLEON
Faintly, from the depths.
                Anyway, keep a fork handy.

PHOBOKLEON
                                        Why a fork?

PHILOKLEON
To fish me out of here before I melt.

PHOBOKLEON
Surveying.
                Let's see—what next? Those shoes are a disgrace.
                Here, take them off. Put on these Spartan slippers.

PHILOKLEON
Spartan slippers?
                                That's enemy produce—contraband!
                They're hostile. They'll corrupt my sole.
                                                I refuse.

PHOBOKLEON
Kneeling to fit the first slipper on.
                Come on, father—quick march, off to Sparta.
                Put your foot in it.

PHILOKLEON
                                What you're doing is a disgrace—
                making me step on Spartan soil. I feel
                as though half of me were deserting to the enemy.

PHOBOKLEON
And the other foot.

PHILOKLEON

              Nope—not that one. The big toe
hates Spartans—gets inflamed every time I turn south.

PHOBOKLEON

Sorry, this is the way things are.

PHILOKLEON

Now completely covered, except for his head,
from which he wipes the sweat.

                          Nothing
is worse than growing old—can't do this,
can't do that. Now I can't even catch cold.

PHOBOKLEON

Will you let me get this slipper on?
                           There we are.
Now, walk as though you had money. You know, a little
insolence, a little lecherousness. Wiggle a little!

PHILOKLEON

Rich, eh?
He tries a tentative strut.
                 Like this? Watch me walk, and tell me
which rich man you think I look like.
He swaggers.

PHOBOKLEON

                       Hmmm.
Hard to say. Rather like a pimple with a bandage on.

PHILOKLEON

What's that, son? Like a pimp? But *which* rich man?
Doesn't matter—I know just the thing—
a bump, and a grind, and a couple of shakes of the tail.

PHOBOKLEON

Fine, just fine. Now, then, to Conversation.
Will you be able to hold your own in weighty
discourse with clever, witty, learned men?

PHILOKLEON

Nobody better.

90

PHOBOKLEON

Doubtfully.

> Well, what would you say? Do you have
> an anecdote, maybe?

PHILOKLEON

> I've got millions.

PHOBOKLEON

> For example?

PHILOKLEON

Well, first there's how they snared the ogress Lamia
and she farted loose; and then there's the one about Little
Kardopion, taking his mother by the . . .

PHOBOKLEON

> No!
Not that! No fairy tales! You'll have to be realistic:
Everyday stories about everyday human beings—
domestic anecdotes—things around the house.

PHILOKLEON

Things around the house? Oh, I get you now.
Like this:
> *Once upon a time a cat and a mouse . . .*

PHOBOKLEON

OF ALL THE GAUCHE, UNLETTERED IDIOTS!—and I quote
(Theogenes said it to another collector of crap!):
Are you going to talk about cats and mice in *Society?*

PHILOKLEON

Sulkily.

What *am* I supposed to tell them?

PHOBOKLEON

> Important things—
stories that confer some dignity, fix some *fashion*
on you as narrator. For instance, tell them how
you were Athens' representative at a festival—you,
and Androkles, and Kleisthenes.

PHILOKLEON

Kleisthenes? I thought you said
no fairy tales. And anyway, I never represented
Athens—except at Paros. Got two obols a day
for that—the same as all the other privates.

PHOBOKLEON

Er—yes. Well, no matter: You've been to Olympia.
Remember? Ah, what a story! You saw Ephoudion,
old and grizzled as he was, hold his own against
young Askondas, wrestling catch-as-catch-can.
Ah, that was a battle, now! Age against youth—
the stag at bay! Tell them of Ephoudion's might—
how, for all his gray hairs, his chest was a brass-bound
barrel, his hands were hammers, his sides were steel,
his breast was bronze, his—

PHILOKLEON

Stop it, son—that's foolish.
He couldn't fight—he couldn't even move.

PHOBOKLEON

Deflated.

Well, that's the clever set's conversation.
We'd better
try something else. Let's have a suggestion from you.
Now, if you're drinking and making society small talk,
what would you tell your hosts was the most manly deed
you performed in those far-off days of your youth?

PHILOKLEON

Most manly?
Most grown-up? Oh, sure—I stole Ergasion's vine-poles.

PHOBOKLEON

Vine-poles? No, no, NO! Didn't you ever
chase a boar, or at least a rabbit, or run
in a relay? What's your most heroic accomplishment?

PHILOKLEON

Heroic? I took a dare once—you know Phaÿllos?

PHOBOKLEON
The Olympic runner?

PHILOKLEON
        That's the one. I took after him—
And I caught him. A close race. Beat him by just two votes—
libel suit. But I was in condition, then.

PHOBOKLEON
Enough!
        Let's accomplish what we can. Lie down,
and learn to be convivial, fit for civilized intercourse.

PHILOKLEON
All ears.

        How do I lie down for *that?* Hurry up!

PHOBOKLEON
                With grace.

PHILOKLEON
Hurling himself onto his back, and assuming,
roughly, the fetal position.
        This what you want?

PHOBOKLEON
        Definitely, irrevocably, NO.

PHILOKLEON
Well, then, *how?*

PHOBOKLEON
Manfully.

        First, extend the knees.
That's it.
        Now, slide the body in supple, liquid curves—
the ones they teach in school—over the tapestries.
Philokleon looks dubiously at his astrakhan. He
becomes more and more confused as Phobokleon
sweeps on.
        Take up a piece of plate and praise it to the skies.
Inspect the ceiling. Marvel at the richly woven
hangings in the hall.

As if to a Waiter.

Water for our hands—over here!

Bring in the tables! And now we dine.

He mimes eating.

And now

the finger-bowls.

He mimes washing.

And now we pour libations.

He mimes pouring and drinking.

PHILOKLEON

That's a dream of a dinner, son—and just as filling.

PHOBOKLEON

Not to be stopped.

The flute-girl gives us a note. Our fellow-guests
are here—Theoros, Aischines, Phanos, and Kleon,
and there's somebody else right by him. Who is it?

He squints and cranes, imitated by Philokleon,
who is still confused.

Oh,

it's Akestor's son.—When you're in *this* sort of company,
father, you have to know your drinking songs.

PHILOKLEON

Oh, I do.

PHOBOKLEON

When the man before you sings a line,
do you know how to top it?

PHILOKLEON

Perfectly.

PHOBOKLEON

Really?

PHILOKLEON

I'm even better than the yodelers up in the hills.

PHOBOKLEON

Well, we'll soon find out. Now, I'll be Kleon,
and I'll start off the "Harmodios." You try to top it.

Sings.

Never again will Athens find . . .

PHILOKLEON

Sings.

. . .a thief like you; *you've stolen her blind.*

PHOBOKLEON

You can't sing *that!* They'd howl you into your grave!
I can hear Kleon now:

"I'LL EXTERMINATE YOU!
EXTIRPATE YOU! EXCISE YOU FROM THE COUNTRY!"

PHILOKLEON

Excellent! Let him threaten—I'll sing another:

O Captain! my Captain! you've sold the bloody sail,
and hocked the mast, and pawned the poop, and traded the after-rail.
The Ship of State is still afloat, but trembles on the brink:
Sit down! Stop throwing your weight around! Do you want the boat to
    SINK?

PHOBOKLEON

Adequate, adequate.

But there's Theoros now, lying

at Kleon's feet. He strokes his hand, and sings:

"Admetos friended Herakles:
his profit was exceeding.
So learn from stories such as these:
be friends with men of breeding."

Do you have a song for that?

PHILOKLEON

A *lyric,* no less:

I'll never be ready
to play the toady
or wear the shackle
of the two-faced jackal.

96

PHOBOKLEON
Now then, after him, Aischines takes it up.
He's a man of colossal culture, mighty in music—
by his own admission. His song, of course, concerns *him:*

> *"Up North, in a song-competition,*
> *I tied with a woman musician.*
> *What money we grossed!*
> *We're Thessaly's toast. . . ."*

PHILOKLEON
> *We boasted it into submission.*

PHOBOKLEON
Well, you *do* understand the way to sing. That's something.
So, now for dinner at Philoktemon's. Which means we'd better
take food.
Turning to the house.
> Hey, boy!
Sosias appears at the door.
> Pack lunch for the two of us.
Sosias retires into the house.

PHILOKLEON
> Lunch?

PHOBOKLEON
Certainly. Philoktemon never serves *food*—it's a *party!*
For once, we're going to get drunk.

PHILOKLEON
> No, son—not that!
Nothing good ever came out of bottles. Just trouble—
Breaking and Entering, Theft, Assault and Battery—
then the morning after, the hangover, those fines to pay . . .
Your wine's a mocker, and mighty expensive, too.

PHOBOKLEON
But not in Society, Father; not with Gentlemen!
Finesse is the word in these circles. You make a gaffe—
a lawsuit? No, it's a simple social lapse,
quickly soothed and smoothed by the intercession of friends;
Conversation leads to Reconciliation.

Or *you* release the tension, with a funny fable
from Aesop, or a Sybaris-story*—a people-fable.
Learn one at the banquet. Then, if something goes wrong,
you tell it, convert the crisis into a joke,
and your accuser will laugh urbanely, release you,
and return to the happy eddy of High Society.

PHILOKLEON
That so? I'd better learn a lot of those fables.
Crime without Punishment. What'll they think of next?

PHOBOKLEON
So it's off to Society! Way for Men of Fashion!
Father and son set off eagerly and exit right,
followed shortly from the house by Sosias, who
carries a heavy lunchbasket.

FIRST SEMICHORUS*
 I thought I was The Champion,
 at dining-out The Best.
 I never dreamed that mincing fop,
 AMYNIAS, could wrest
 away my Prize for Guestmanship;
 he somehow didn't seem equipped,
   because he doesn't EAT,
   not Amynias.

 His manners were disgraceful.
 Leogoras, the glutton,
 invited him to gorge himself
 from muffins down to mutton,
 and you know what that shittard *did?*
 He came—but *wouldn't eat!* Instead,
   he fiddled with a quince—
   that Amynias!

 He differed from his goodly host—
 the fundamental gaffe!
 But now he's done a sharp reverse
 and made me eat my laugh.
 He went upon an embassy
 to check on things in Thessaly
   and carried off my crown,
   did Amynias!

Up North, he didn't grace the Rich
and Mighty with his presence;
he ate and drank exclusively
with greasy, stinking peasants
who served him NOTHING!

                              What a coup!
I take my napkin off to you,
              you greasy, stinking, starveling
              Slob, Amynias!

FIRST KORYPHAIOS
Is Automenes in the audience?

                              Congratulations, sir—
you've been chosen FATHER OF THE YEAR!

                                   Take a bow, sir!—
Three fine sons, unsurpassed in their service to ART!
We all know and love Son #1, Arignotos the Harper—
a harper's harper, I might say—unmatched in music.
And Son #2, Automenes Jr., the eminent Actor—
well, gentlemen, words fail me—what indescribable skill!
But it's Son #3, Ariphrades, who staggers the senses—
what an endowment of Natural Talent! Would you believe it,
gentlemen, that slip of a boy, completely untaught (his father
swears he never took a lesson in his life), devised,
by his own unaided wits, a method of Oral Expression
which enables him daily to visit the tightest spots in the city
and come off top dog through the use of his golden tongue?

                                        Best Wishes,
Automenes, Father of Three:
                    a HARPER,
                              an ACTOR,
                                   a PERVERT!

SECOND SEMICHORUS*

        . . . .

SECOND KORYPHAIOS
To rectify the record:

                    Rumor has it that I, the author,*
have kissed and made up with Kleon. It alleges that he scratched and
    badgered
until I buried the hatchet.

                    A canard. Here are the facts:

I found I was fighting alone.

When the Tanner dragged me to court,
I expected popular support from the folks who flocked to the case.
And what did I get? Laughs.

He peeled my skin off in strips;
I howled—and the spectators roared.

Dimly, I saw that my backing
was only a comedian's claque, political voyeurs assembled
to see me prodded until I produced some tasty billingsgate.
Faced with such odds, I changed my tactics—played the ape,
flattered Kleon a bit.

But what does he think today,
now that this docile doormat is pulling the rug from under him?

*Sosias, battered, bloody, bruised, and torn, reels
in from the right, watched with amazement and
consternation by the Chorus. With a great deal of
agony, he manages to stagger to center stage, where
he suddenly straightens up, advances, and speaks in
a relatively untortured tone.*

SOSIAS
I should like to take the present opportunity
to congratulate all you turtles, wherever you are.
Oh, happy creatures cradled in horny carapaces,
triply serene in solid siding on your ribs,
what a consummate genius was yours, to roof
your backs with tile, shelter from blows!—Whereas,
I'M BLACK AND BLUE! MY RIBS ARE CLUBBED ALL TO
    HELL!

FIRST KORYPHAIOS
What's the trouble, boy? (Since common usage
decrees that "boy" refers to one who suffers
beatings, be he old or young.*)—But what's the trouble?

SOSIAS
The trouble's that old disaster Philokleon—what else?
Nobody could possibly get that drunk; but *he* managed.
He beat the cream of Athenian alcoholism—easy!
What a party! Every local lush, lecher,
loud-mouth, pervert, bully-ragger—they were all there:
Hippyllos, Antiphon, Lykon, Lysistratos, Theophrastos,
that slimy dancer Phrynichos* and his pansy friends.

100

But Philokleon won the Degeneracy Prize hands down,
going away. And quickly, too. He filled himself up
and went completely wild, treating us all
to an exhibition of kicks, jumps, brays, farts—
an ass at a banquet of barley. Then he beat the hell
out of me: "BOY!" he'd shout—WHOP!

                                    "BOY!"

                                    WHOP!

Then Lysistratos saw him, and sharpened up his tongue:
"Hey, old man," he said, "what are you? A new way
to spice up leftovers? No, you look more like a jackass
loose in the pea-patch." But Philokleon brayed right back.
He compared Lysistratos—now, let me get this straight—
to a locust—who'd lost—the fig leaves—off his old overcoat—
". . . just like that playwright Sthenelos sheared of his props!"
No one knew what he meant, but they clapped like mad—
except Theophrastos. He's a wit. He sneered.
The old man charged right up. "What call have *you* got,"
he bawled, "to be so snotty and hoity-toity?
You suck the socks of every rich man in town!"
Then he got sort of insulting. He went right down
the guest-list, calling names like a mule-skinner,
all the time babbling these . . . *fables,* he called them. Just words—
no plot, no point, no place in the conversation.
Finally, when he's absolutely stinking, he leaves,
reels off for home—and clobbers everyone he meets
with his torch. And what's even worse than that . . .

Shouts, thumps, and crashes from offstage right.

                                  Oh-oh!

That's him—I know that stagger by ear. Goodbye.
Beatings are one thing I do very well without.

He limps quickly and painfully into the house.
After a short pause, a curious procession enters
from the right. It is led by Philokleon, raving drunk
—a condition in which he remains for the rest of
the play. He carries a torch in one hand and
clutches at a stark naked flute-girl, whom he has
stolen from the party, with the other. They are
followed, at a very slight distance, by an irate band
of banquet-guests, small tradesmen, etc., whom
Philokleon has managed to outrage in one way or
another during the course of the evening. He keeps
this group at bay by brandishing his torch at it
occasionally.

PHILOKLEON

Singing a drunken variation on a wedding march.

Take up the torch! Hic!

Here comesh the bride!

Some—body behind me

will have his hide fried!

Here comesh the bride!

Hold high the torch! Hic!

He waves the torch at the followers.

Haul your asses out of here

or I'll scorch you in the crotch! Hic!

He makes a sudden lunge. The crowd shrinks back.
He turns. The crowd presses nervously toward him.
One guest from the banquet advances.

GUEST

You're not going to get away with this! You'll pay!
Tomorrow! And being a minor is no damn excuse!
Breaking and Entering! Theft! Assault and Battery!
We'll all come down together and SUBPOENA you!

PHILOKLEON

A real SUBPOENA—for ME?

Gee!

Shaking his torch.

Thash ancient history—

don't let me

hear any more

about COURTS!

He jabs at the crowd with the torch.

Parry!

Thrust!

He moves back and squeezes the flute-girl
experimentally.

Here's the stuff!

He squeezes again.

Moshtes' an' beshtes'—

He gives a third, magnificent squeeze, and
addresses the heavens.

SCREW JUSTICE!!!

Turning to the crowd again.

Git! Where's that lawyer?

The guest who brought the accusation hurriedly
buries himself in the crowd.

Everybody out of here!

He swings the torch wildly. The crowd stampedes
back the way it has come and exits. Philokleon
watches with alcoholic satisfaction, then turns to
the flute-girl and motions her to the front door.
He gazes at the upper window.

All right, honey-bee, first thing to do is get in.
You mount—upsy daisy!

He looks at the window again.

'Shtoo high—need a rope.

Shows his phallus.

Here'sh one—grab this.

Careful—that rope'sh pretty rotten—
but a little friction—hic!—won't hurt it any.
C'mon, you little cockchafer, chafe away!

The flute-girl shakes her head.

Now look, is this gratitude? You know those guests
were just about to make you open up and play
that Lesbian lay—but I put the snatch on you.
You could do's mush for me. Or lend me a hand—

The flute-girl is unmoved. He tries the sulks.

But hell, you won't—won't even try. I know you:
you're juss a tease—you'll make thish come unshcrewed.
Thash what you did to everyone elsh. —Look,
I'll tell you what. You be nice t' me *now*—
real nice—you know—and when that son of mine dies,
I'll buy your contract, all legal—and you can be
my concubine. How's that, you queen of a quim? All right?
Don't worry; I've got money, but it's all in trusht—
I'm not of age: can't touch an obol—just yet.
How's about it?*

The flute-girl smiles, nods, and sidles up to him. He
puts an arm around her, suddenly withdraws it, then
replaces it cautiously, looking around warily.

We'll have to be careful—I'm WATCHED!
It's that moss-backed son—won't let me out of his sight.
Oooh, he's mean! And stingy?—Did you ever eat *half*
of a caraway seed? That's what he serves *me!*
Anyway, he's afraid I'll get corrupted or something.
I'm an only father, you know.

—Oh-oh! Here he comes,
fast. I get the feeling we're the target.
Here! Quick—hold this torch and make like a statue.

He needs a hazing, and I'm just the boy to do it.
I'll use the trick he tried on me before
my initiation. Be a brother to your son, as the saying goes.

He hands the torch to the flute-girl, who freezes into
an appropriate attitude. He then adjusts his mantle
and assumes an innocent expression just in time to
greet Phobokleon as he rushes in from the right.

PHOBOKLEON
Angry both at the theft of a flute-girl and at the
failure of a theory of father-raising.
There you are, you Senile Delinquent! You old
Bandersnatch! The Great Lover himself—too limp
for Rigor Mortis! You won't get away with this!

PHILOKLEON
Hungry, son? Do you want a nice fried lawsuit
with plenty of sauce?

PHOBOKLEON
This is terrible, Father!
Fun's fun—but you can't steal the flutist from a feast!

PHILOKLEON
Flutist? What flutist? You're babbling, boy. Looks like
you fell right off your pedestal and cracked your head.

PHOBOKLEON
Pointing at the flute-girl.
You know perfectly well what flutist—THAT ONE!

PHILOKLEON
That's no flutist, son. It's a public fixture.

PHOBOKLEON
A fixture?

PHILOKLEON
A torch. They burn them to the gods.
He knocks Phobokleon's hands away from the girl.
Be reverent, son.

PHOBOKLEON
A *torch?*

PHILOKLEON

> Yup. New model—

see the handy-dandy slit? Fits anywhere.

PHOBOKLEON

What are these?

PHILOKLEON

> Additional handles—reduce fatigue.

PHOBOKLEON

What's this black patch in the middle?

PHILOKLEON

> That patch? Pitch.

Get one of these torches hot and out it comes.

PHOBOKLEON

What's this back here? An ass if I ever saw one!

PHILOKLEON

That's a knot in the wood. Interesting formation.

PHOBOKLEON

A knot? What are you talking about?
To the flute-girl.

> —Come here, you!

He starts to drag her off right.

PHILOKLEON
Grabbing the flute-girl and tugging.

Hey, son, what are you up to?

PHOBOKLEON

> More than you are.

I'm taking this girl away from you and back
to the banquet. Face facts, Father: You're worn out,
used up, rotten. *You* can't do a thing!

PHILOKLEON

Now, wait a minute. You listen to me!
Phobokleon, surprised, stops.

I represented Athens at the Olympics,
and there I saw Ephoudion, old and grizzled,
fight young Askondas and hold his own—and more!
That old fellow lifted up his fist—like this—

He raises his right hand high.

and brought it down hard—like this—

*He strikes Phobokleon a terrific blow on top of
the head, and knocks him down.*

and felled the whelp—

like that!

*He quickly ushers the flute-girl into the house,
shouting over his shoulder.*

Watch out—next time you get a black eye!*

PHOBOKLEON
Staggering to his feet as his father returns.

By god—he finally learned the Olympia bit!

*Myrtia, a proprietress of a bakery-shop, enters
holding an empty breadbasket in one hand and
dragging Chairephon, a tall, cadaverous man who
is to be her witness, by the other. She has to keep
chivvying Chairephon, who is rather unhappy about
the whole affair.*

MYRTIA
To Chairephon.

Come ON! Stand right here, please!

HERE, idiot!

There he is! There's the man who ruined me!

*Phobokleon starts suddenly, and looks wonder-
ingly at Philokleon.*

He beat me up with his torch,

She brandishes the basket.

and knocked *this* over—
squashed the bread—ten obols—and the cover—four more.

PHOBOKLEON
Aside, to Philokleon.

Do you see what you've done—you and your wine?
All the troubles and lawsuits back again!

PHILOKLEON
Why, no, son. All we need is an anecdote—

106

Conversation leads to Reconciliation.
You just watch me reconcile this old bag here.

MYRTIA

Oh, you'll pay, you will! You won't get off so easy!
No, sir, no one can ruin the stock of Myrtia,
daughter and successor of Ankylion and Sostrate—
an old, established firm—and not suffer!

PHILOKLEON

Listen to me, woman. I want to tell you
a pretty little fable.

MYRTIA

Not me, you don't!

PHILOKLEON

Aesop was coming home from dinner one evening
when he was barked at by a shaggy, drunken bitch.
He moves closer to Myrtia. She recoils.
And Aesop said,
Yelling in Myrtia's ear.

"YOU BITCH, YOU BITCH, YOU BITCH!
It'd be a good idea for you to trade
that nasty tongue in on some grain—YOU BITCH!"

MYRTIA

Slander, too? Well! I don't know what your name is,
but I'll summon you before the Board of Trade
to face the charge of Damaging Merchandise. And here's—
Tugging at Chairephon.
and here's my witness—
Tugging again, this time with success.
(come ON!)—
Chairephon!

PHILOKLEON

You don't mean that. Here's another; see how it strikes you.
The poet Lasos was competing with Simonides once.
Know what he said? He said: "I couldn't care less."

MYRTIA
Oh, he did, did he!

And here's old Chairephon. Hi, there!

Chairephon cowers behind Myrtia.

Pasty-Face a witness for Rose-Red here—

He indicates Myrtia, who is crimson with fury.

that's quite a match. You look like Ino, hanging
by the feet. Of Euripides. Begging him not to cast her
in one of his plays.

*Myrtia grabs Chairephon and stalks off without a
word. Philokleon, beatific, watches them leave, then
turns back to the house. Phobokleon continues
watching for a moment.*

PHOBOKLEON

Here comes somebody else.
Looks like another subpoena; he's brought his witness.

*Beaten and bruised, there enters haltingly a Man
who looks like Euripides.* He is followed by a
Witness, who carries stylus and tablet.*

THE MAN WHO LOOKS LIKE EURIPIDES

AGONY! MALAISE! ALACKADAISY!

Grisard, attend:

I'll criminate thee with ATROCITY!

PHOBOKLEON

Atrocity? Oh, *no!*
See here, Sir—set whatever penalty you wish,
and I'll pay it for him, and thank you in the bargain.

PHILOKLEON

It's my place, son. I'm overjoyed to make restitution.
He's right—I admit Assault and Battery.

To the Man Who Looks Like Euripides, sweetly.

—Sir,

please step over here.

*The Man Who Looks Like Euripides complies,
groaning. The Witness follows.*

I desire to be your friend
in perpetuity. Can't we settle this out of Court?
Will you allow me to fix the amount of the fine
I'll have to pay, or would *you* prefer to set it?

THE MAN WHO LOOKS LIKE EURIPIDES
Pronounce the escheat. Fain would I eschew
dispute and suit.
                    —OOOO!

PHILOKLEON
                                        A man of Sybaris
fell out of a chariot once and smashed his skull
to smithereens; he was no horseman. A friend of his
came up and said, "The cobbler should stick to his last."
In your case, friend, it means you should hobble off fast
to the Free Clinic.
He knocks the tablet out of the Witness's hands,
breaking it. Phobokleon buries his head in his hands.

PHOBOKLEON
                    If you have one virtue, it's consistency.

THE MAN WHO LOOKS LIKE EURIPIDES
To his Witness, who stands stupidly holding
his stylus.
        Impress in mind's inmost recess these insults!
He starts to leave.

PHILOKLEON
Don't run off. Listen: In Sybaris once, a woman
smashed a hedgehog.*

THE MAN WHO LOOKS LIKE EURIPIDES
To his Witness.
                            Attest that witless thrust!

PHILOKLEON
Just what the hedgehog did—it called a witness.
And the woman of Sybaris said, "You'd show more sense,
if you forgot this witness-business entirely,
and ran as quick as you could to buy a bandage."

THE MAN WHO LOOKS LIKE EURIPIDES
Indulge thy raging, till thou'rt led to judging!
OUCH!
He limps off, groaning, followed by the Witness.
As Philokleon watches in satisfaction, Phobokleon
sneaks softly behind him.

PHOBOKLEON

In a low voice which is not heard by Philokleon.
> You simply can't stay here any longer.
> I'll just lift you up and. . . .

He scoops the old man up in his arms.

PHILOKLEON
> What are you doing?

PHOBOKLEON
> Me?
> I'm carrying you inside. If I leave you here,
> every witness in town will be used up in half an hour.

He strides for the door, lugging his father.

PHILOKLEON
Once Aesop was accused . . .

PHOBOKLEON
> I couldn't care less!

PHILOKLEON
. . . by the people of Delphi. They said he'd stolen a vase
that belonged to Apollo. But he told them the story
about the beetle.
> Once upon a time, a beetle. . . .

PHOBOKLEON
Reaching the door at last.
> I'll put an end to you *and* your beetles, by God!

*The house-door closes behind them. Philokleon can
still be heard babbling his fable.*

FIRST SEMICHORUS
> I envy Philokleon's luck,
> so happily arranged.
> His rough, and rude, and often crude
> mode of life has changed.

[*Crashes and yells from the house.**]

> He's learned the theory, has it pat;
> now comes the execution.
> He turns to Ease and Luxuries—
> a Total Revolution!

[*The flute-girl appears at the upper window, screams,
and disappears.*]

110

But will he really wish to shift
from Habit's well-worn routes?
Dame Nature's hard to disregard—
will he join in New Pursuits?

[*The door of the house bursts open, and out flies
the flute-girl, chased by Philokleon. He pursues
her around the stage.*]

Others change, for New Ideas
accomplish more than kicks.
With a gentle jog, the Oldest Dog
will gladly learn New Tricks!

[*Phobokleon and the slaves (Xanthias excepted)
hurry from the house and chase Philokleon. The
flute-girl escapes, but back into the house.
Phobokleon and the slaves catch Philokleon and
re-enter, carrying him.*]

SECOND SEMICHORUS

All men of sensibility
will join me, I feel sure,
as now I raise a song of praise
to the Author of this Cure.

[*More crashes and yells from the house.*]

All Hail to Philokleon's son!
Exalt him to the skies!
Did ever lad so love his dad?
Was ever boy so wise?

[*The flute-girl, screaming again, appears at the
upper window. She is in the clutches of Philokleon,
who is in turn being beaten by Phobokleon with
the torch. The tableau disappears suddenly.*]

What manners! What demeanor! What
behavior in a boy!
What soft address! What gentleness!
It made me melt with joy!

[*The door bursts open, and the trio emerges: The
flute-girl, chased by Philokleon, chased by
Phobokleon with the torch.*]

And in debate, this paragon
inspired his parent's notions
to Things Above, by Filial Love—
the noblest of emotions!

ALL HAIL, PHOBOKLEON!

[*Philokleon catches the flute-girl. Phobokleon
trips and drops the torch. Philokleon scoops it up,
throws the flute-girl over his shoulder, and beats
his howling son before him into the house.*]

Xanthias emerges from the house, shaking his head.

XANTHIAS

Dionysos, what a mess! Some god's been playing stagehand,
meddling with the set. The house is an absolute snarl.
It's the old man. After all these years, he took
a drink, and heard one note from the flute—and bang!
the combination sent him right out of his head.
                                        To his feet.
He's mad, but now he's mad for dancing. Been at it
all night long. No end in sight. Except his.
By now, he's worked through all those antique dances
that Thespis taught his choruses a century ago,
and claims he's ready for the Modern School. Performers
in tragedies today, like Phrynichos and all his ilk,
are feeble old fogies, he says: they can't match *him!*
He's even threatened to come out here in a while
and show the young men up by dancing them down
at all their own steps.* Talk about the light fantastic!

He sits down, leaning against the door.

PHILOKLEON

*From behind the door, declaiming Euripidean
fustian.*
            Who couches before the courtyard portals?
The door rattles. Xanthias jumps away.

XANTHIAS

To the audience.
            You're about to witness an outbreak of plague.
*He runs off.**

PHILOKLEON
            Ho, there! Unshoot the bolts!

The door bursts open, and Philokleon jigs forth.
He is rehearsing the violent movements of a gro-
tesquely acrobatic dance. After him, sad and
defeated, comes Phobokleon.

'Tis time!
The gambado commences!

PHOBOKLEON
Wearily.

And sanity ends.

PHILOKLEON
Let's see. How does Phrynichos do it?
Suiting action to words, as far as possible.
He begins with a flourish, a sudden convulsive
contortion of the ribs! A blare from the nostrils!
A ruffle and scrunch of splintered vertebrae!

PHOBOKLEON
How are you treating it? Hellebore? Hemlock?

PHILOKLEON
He coils in a crouch like an angry cock . . .

PHOBOKLEON
If that doesn't work, we could stone you, of course.

PHILOKLEON
. . . then lashes a kick that scrapes the stars!

PHOBOKLEON
And his ass gapes wide to the spectators' stares.

PHILOKLEON
You'd better watch out for yourself!
He revolves and jumps more and more wildly.
Phobokleon moves out of the way.

And now
the final pirouette, the supple, unsocketed
whizzing and whirring of a dislocated femur!
He spins and kicks more frantically, coming to a
stop before Phobokleon.
Pretty good, huh?

114

PHOBOKLEON

Positively NO! Utter Delirium!

PHILOKLEON

Paying no attention, he advances to the audience.

An Announcement:

To All Performers from the Tragic Stage
Who Make Any Pretense to Excellence in the Dance, I Fling
a Blanket Challenge: COME UP AND COMPETE WITH *ME!*

Silence.

—Anybody? Nobody?

PHOBOKLEON

Here comes one—but that's all.

A small dancer, dressed as a crab, scurries on stage.

PHILOKLEON

What happened to *him?*

PHOBOKLEON

Heredity. He's the son of Karkinos*
the dancer—you know what a crusty old crab *he* is.

PHILOKLEON

That's no competition. A downbeat or two from me,
and he's done. Cooked. Dished. He'll make a nice mouthful,
the way he makes hash of the rhythm.

A second crab-clad dancer scurries up.

PHOBOKLEON

I wouldn't have your luck.
What bait are you using? You caught another crab—
his brother.

PHILOKLEON

I didn't mean for this to be a dinner-dance.
I wanted a ballet.

PHOBOKLEON

Looking off.

You've got a buffet—three crabs.

PHILOKLEON
Three?

115

PHOBOKLEON

Well, here comes another son of Karkinos.

A very tiny crab-dancer scurries on.

PHILOKLEON

What's this creeping thing? A trivet? A spider?

PHOBOKLEON

That's the youngest—the shrimp of the family. They all
act, but he writes. That makes it a real tragedy.

PHILOKLEON

O Karkinos, how you must jump for joy at your offspring!
And the whole bunch of little bounders has dropped on *us!*

To Phobokleon.

I must enter the lists. To celebrate my victory in the dance,
fix something for my opponents. A sauce. Use plenty of capers.
And now to see crabbed youth compete with age.

*He moves to the center of the stage to begin the
dance.*

FIRST KORYPHAIOS

To the Chorus.

All right, men, let's pull back a little and give them room.
We don't want to be in the way when they try those whip-top spins.

*The Chorus forms a large semicircle, in which
the Sons of Karkinos begin their wild dance.
Philokleon waits.*

ENTIRE CHORUS

To the Sons of Karkinos.

Aloft! ye crustacean lords of gyration,
eccentrically tracing your dizzy descent from the
undulant loins of the God of the Ocean!
O Arthropod paladins, sires of Circuitry!
Scuttle and pound on the sterile salt strand!
Scurry and stamp! O ye kinsmen to shrimp!

In wild revolution, in whirligig tension,
enjumble and fumble the force of a tragedy!
Mount to the climax with pouncing distortion,
then bound to the sky to confound the peripety!
Flick with your kick the shriek of a claque,
engulfing the plays in brainless applause.

To Philokleon as he spins into the dance.

> In giddy glissade, let vertigo reign! Embellish the eddy
> and spiral your shins to the stars!

*To the Sons of Karkinos, as Philokleon spins
among them.*

> Be bobbins, and reel to make ready
> your master's turbinate triumph! Oh, wheel to the liege of the sea—
> who scuds and unsettles those lords of the stage, his children three!

*At this point the dancing contest turns into a rout.
Philokleon, spinning and kicking, attacks in turn
the three crabs and pursues them in a mad circle.
The Chorus addresses the maelstrom plaintively.*

> *Please* lead us off. You can keep up the dance if you must, but *hurry!*
> It's not that innovations annoy us, but we *do* have a worry:
> We admit that many actors have had the chance to dismiss
> the Chorus by using a final dance—
>   BUT NEVER A DANCE LIKE
>   *THIS!*

*Still gyrating and jumping, Philokleon pursues the
three Sons of Karkinos off-stage; the Chorus and
cast follow, dancing just as madly as their leaders.*

Notes

page 9. *Korybants:* Priests of the goddess Kybele, whose rites were distinguished by wild dancing.

11. *that tanner Kleon:* The demagogue owned a leather factory, and Aristophanes never forgot it.

11. *Theoros was a sapsucker:* There is a play here in the Greek on Alkibiades' lisp, which substituted *l* for *r*, so that Theoros has the head of a *kolax* "flatterer" rather than a *korax* "raven." Rogers' *raven-cwaven* alternation is the nearest English. Better to forget the lisp.

13. *CROAK:* In the Greek, a play on the common billingsgate phrase *es korakas* "To the crows!"—i.e., "Go to hell!"

13. *thanks to luck:* By virtue of his victory over the Spartans at Sphakteria in the summer of 425.

14. *Not too refined and dainty for you, of course:* The first of a string of gibes at the intelligence of the audience. Also note that a good number of the points of the preceding program are contradicted in the course of the play. Thus slapstick abounds, Kleon is hit at every opportunity, and, if the scholiast is correct, Euripides appears, thoroughly worked over.

14. *SOSIAS:* As noted in the Introduction (p. 5), the texts of Coulon and Cantarella assign the entire address to the audience here to the slave whose name is Xanthias. I think this bad philology and bad dramaturgy, and have gone back to the texts of Rogers, Van Leeuwen, and Starkie, who break up the speech with Sosias' backchat.

15. *Long Line:* Athenian juries, in certain cases, established the penalty—or rather chose between one proposed by the defendant and one proposed by the plaintiff. The choice of the individual juror was indicated by a line drawn by a stylus on a wax tablet: short for minimum, long for maximum. The Stings which the Chorus wear would appear to be enlarged representations of this stylus.

16. *PHOBOKLEON:* The Greek name is Bdelykleon, "Loathe-Kleon," which is under two disadvantages for an English-speaking audience, i.e., it is at once meaningless and unpronounceable.

peach-wood: In Greek, *sykinou*, "fig-wood," with the consequent play on *sykophantēs*, "informer."

23. *Phrynichos:* The famous Athenian tragic poet of an earlier day. The allusion here may be specifically to his *Phoenician Women,* presented in 476.

25. *wasps' stings:* The location of these stings—front or back?—has occasioned some little discussion, and my solution may seem unattractive, particularly to those who deny the presence of the phallus in Aristophanes' plays. I only urge that objectors (1) look at a wasp, (2) consider that this sting, in the play, is (or was) not only the seat of the Chorus' might but of their manhood, (3) remember that "tail" is the whole lower end of the torso. (It is curious to conjecture what might have become of this play had Aristophanes known that the sting is borne only by the *female* wasp.)

26. *squeezed Sicily dry:* Laches' peculations are conjectural. He *did* lose a battle at Leontini in Sicily in 427 and undergo survey thereafter, but seems to have avoided conviction, since he fought at Delion in 424 and established a truce there in 423. Whether this refers to the former survey or a current one is unknown; it may only refer to a possible one, since the opposition between Laches, an oligarch, and Kleon, mainstay of "the people," would have been drawn on strictly party lines.

28. *Secret Agent in Samos:* A reference to the unsuccessful revolt of that island from enforced Athenian democracy in 440.

28. *a traitor from Thrace:* The Thracian cities Amphipolis and Eion were betrayed by their inhabitants to the Spartan general Brasidas in 424.

30. *Proxenides' bluster:* This man and Aischines were two well-known boasters, the Athenian equivalent for "hot air" being "smoke." (Which lies at the bottom of the translation "smudgepot" in line 151 above.)

31. *our Navy's going to pot:* Nothing has been—or will be—said about the Navy, or about Demeter's legislation in the parallel accusation in 379 below. The Chorus is pathologically suspicious, and can credit no one with good motives.

33. *Demeter's legislation:* One would expect the Chorus to say "Demeter's mysteries." The confusion is, of course, Aristophanes' way of indicating to what extent religion and politics have been confused by these litigious old men. At least, this is the usual explanation.

34. *Lykos my Master:* Son of the legendary King Pandion of Athens; his statue, in the form of a wolf (*lykos*) was set, we are told, before each court.

36. *and hold it high, Boys:* From this point until the Debate, the Chorus' actions proceed from an adolescent enthusiasm shakily reared on their senile decrepitude. To evoke this, I have translated here on the pattern of that archetypal fight song which daily greeted prepubescent Ameri-

cans from their radios in the late 1930's and early 1940's—the hymn to Hudson High School which prefaced the exploits of "Jack Armstrong, the All-American Boy."

page 43. *Brasidas:* Because of his recent and threatening victories in Thrace, the Spartan general was a name for the popular party to beat the conservatives with in 422.

43. *SUBVERSIVE:* A closer modern American equivalent for *synomotes* than the literal "conspirator," as "dictatorship" is nearer to *tyrannis* than "tyranny."

49. *his daughter:* The usual pun on *choiros* ("pig" and "female genitalia") that is so thoroughly employed in *Acharnians* 764 ff.

50. *Flee-onymos:* The Greek gives *Kolakonymos,* a punning compound of *kolax* (flatterer) and Kleonymos. Since Kleonymos was also a notorious coward (see, e.g., Xanthias' dream about the eagle, p. 10), Flee-onymos seemed a permissible liberty.

50. *silence from Phobokleon:* An attempt to supply some sort of a joke that seems to have been lost when knowledge of Euphemios (Euphemides?) disappeared. He was probably of the same moral stamp as Theoros—but this is obviously the scholiast's conjecture, based on this passage. Phobokleon, of course, *does* know Theoros.

56. *paying tribute to Athens:* One thousand tributaries seems a considerable overstatement, more than three times the actual figure. But Phobokleon, or Aristophanes, may have another method of counting than modern scholars.

56. *you can have Euboia:* Perikles, in 445, planted Athenian colonists on this grain-fertile island, and promise of the same became a pie-in-the-sky maneuver for the demagogues who came after him.

63. *chamber pot:* A false solution to the problem, but one with better comic sense than having the son produce a shrine. Philokleon's comparison between this and Kleonymos in the original—that Lykos has no shield either —helps the solution not at all. But it must have been pertinent, and I have tried to change it to something that might work.

65. *Chowhound:* In Greek, *Labēs* "Grab"—a pun on the general Laches, as the plaintiff (here "Fleahound") is *Kyōn* "Dog"—a pun on Kleon. The proper-name pun is not worth straining English, especially since Laches' trial is conjectural. Aristophanes' technique here is instructive of his whole approach. Most of the time, a delicate ambiguity is preserved: Chowhound, a dog, could equally well be a general. But at certain points, particularly at the testimony of the Cheese-Grater, the allegory breaks through, and the dogginess nearly disappears.

74. *to old Thoukydides once:* See *Acharnians,* 703 ff.

77. *Harden not your hearts, but melt it in mercy:* The syntactical apogee of Phobokleon's perplexity—is his father one man or a panel of jurors?

page 81. *into others' mouths:* Those of Philonides and Kallistratos, who produced Aristophanes' first plays. See *Clouds* 503 ff.

81. *who shall be nameless:* The rival comedian Eupolis.

82. *first performance:* Under his own name—*The Knights* of 424.

82. *informers:* Thus many critics identify the demons, presuming they were thus attacked in the *Barges* (*Holkades*), presented in 423. Others follow the scholiast and say the demons are the sophists lampooned in *The Clouds.* But the rather tortured Greek seems fairly clear in one thing: This is something which occurred *before* the production of *The Clouds.*

85. *the coming of the Persians:* The battles of Salamis and Marathon are mingled in the following account.

86. *the Archon's court, the Eleven's Court, the converted Odeion:* Three different tribunals: the court of the eponymous archon; the court of the Eleven (concerned with theft and police matters generally); and the Odeion, occasionally taken over to settle litigation arising from the grain-trade.

98. *Sybaris-story:* A conventionalized anecdote, purporting to have taken place in the city of Sybaris in southern Italy. These Sybaritic fables used human characters rather than animals, as in the fables of Aesop.

98. *FIRST SEMICHORUS:* This ode, a very crabbed bit of Greek on which no two commentators seem to agree, has been expanded to show how it may have meant *something.* The solution proposed, that Amynias is censured here for being a starveling, fits the Greek and the situation here, though it supplements rather than complements the information we have in *The Clouds* about this (or another?) Amynias. I have avoided conjecture about the politics involved, though firm theories abound. Here, as elsewhere in Aristophanes, precise hypotheses proliferate in direct proportion to the opacity of the passage.

99. *SECOND SEMICHORUS:* We have lost the antistrophe and the beginning of the speech here given to the Second Koryphaios.

99. *the author:* Probably. The allusion can hardly, considering *The Acharnians* and *The Knights,* be to the (probable) legal action taken by Kleon after *The Babylonians;* it may be some action or threat that followed those two plays, and led indirectly to Aristophanes' abandonment of political attacks in *The Clouds.*

100. *old or young:* A pun on *pais* "boy" and *paiein* "beat" underlies this Euripidean sententiousness.

100. *Phrynichos:* This reference to the other Phrynichos, the contemporary dancer, is clearly to set up the final scene.

103. *How's about it?:* I here abandon the hics! and thickening of sounds. Philokleon remains just as drunk.

106. *next time you get a black eye:* The manuscripts and scholia, as usual, furnish no information about the outcome of this skirmish. It is only fair

to note that editors and commentators, if they deign to discuss stage-action, are eager to balance the scales of morality—and accordingly award both victory and flute-girl to the virtuous son. I can only say that their choice deprives Philokleon's speech here of any motivation or meaning.

page 108. *A Man who looks like Euripides:* So a scholiast names him. Nearly every modern editor rejects this, though it is not the sort of thing that a scholiast would imagine on his own. The most telling argument against the tragedian's appearance is that he does not talk in the fustian that Aristophanes normally employs for him. I have changed his remarks into equivalent fustian, not to avoid the argument, but to supply a modern audience with something like the original effect—which, I think, was purely visual: an easily recognizable mask to identify the tragedian, here "worked over again" most violently.

109. *hedgehog:* In Greek, *echinos,* not only the animal, but a vase, and one associated with courtroom practice. But the straight translation seems to have the required degree of insanity, so I have let it stand.

110. *from the house:* The stage directions here are strictly *exempli causa,* the responsibility (or irresponsibility) of the translator. They have as their aim, however, something serious: To try to point out the comment that is here made by what is probably Aristophanes' most insipid stasimon, violently dislocated. It logically fits after the scene of preparation for the banquet, after line 1264—which is where Van Leeuwen, for one, "replaces" it. But had that been its original location, what ancient editor would have been such an idiot as to move it in the first place? No one but the author, I think, could have put it here—and he did it, not out of clumsiness, or a desire to insert another scene, but calculatingly. Coming as it does after the presentation of the reformed Philokleon, turned young, drunk, and disgusting, bait for the courtroom himself, it underlines, *per contra,* the utter defeat of Phobokleon's altruism. Further, its very flatness almost demands spectacle. Finally, though most commentators banish the flute-girl from the scene early, we know from the final scene that someone was playing the flute inside. Q. E. D.—quite shakily.

113. *at all their own steps:* The controversy over this last scene seems to have been settled by Roos's excellent work, *Die tragische Orchestik im Zerrbild der altattischen Komodie* (Stockholm, 1951). Simply, this is a satirical fling at the excesses of the "New School" of tragic dancing, which specialized in hyperathletic leaps and bounds to no apparent purpose—at least from Aristophanes' conservative viewpoint. The final song has been expanded in translation at the end of this scene to try to show the accomplishment: the gaudy wildness which obscures and ruins tragedy. I have not followed Roos' conclusions as to the nature of Philokleon's dance—a wild, drunkenly lascivious dance normally confined to the late hours of wild parties—but this is simply to let the pseudo-tragic state-

ment work. Anyone hardy enough to attempt this play is perfectly free to insert bumps and grinds at will, provided that the result is both funny and somewhat disgusting; Philokleon's victory is also his degradation.

113. *He runs off:* In most texts, Xanthias has most, if not all, of the lines here given to Phobokleon—a good way to send a scene teetering on the brink of meaninglessness right off the edge.

115. *Karkinos:* A tragic poet, upon the literal meaning of whose name ("the crab") the entire following dance scene is based.

Glossary

ADMETOS: Legendary king of Pherai in Thessaly befriended by the hero Herakles. He is a major figure in Euripides' *Alkestis* and the subject of an Attic drinking song.

AESOP, AISOPOS: Flourished ca. 570 B.C. The author of a famous collection of animal fables.

AGORA: The main marketplace of Athens, used for holding trials, public debates, and the transaction of business.

AISCHINES: A henchman of Kleon (q.v.) and a notorious braggart. His nickname was "Smoke."

AIXONE: A deme of Attika, birthplace of the general Laches (q.v.).

AJAX, AIAS: Son of Telamon and Greek hero of the Trojan War. In the contest for the armor of Achilles, he lost to Odysseus and went mad in consequence. Dishonored, he fell upon his sword and died.

ALKIBIADES: An Athenian politician (ca. 450-404) of great ability and brilliance. Of aristocratic Alkmaeonid descent, he was related to Perikles and was, for some time, a devoted disciple of Sokrates. Distinguished by wealth, birth, and spectacular personal beauty, he spent his youth in lavish display and debauchery (Pheidippides in *Clouds* has been thought to be a caricature of Alkibiades).

AMYNIAS: Son of Pronapes and one of Strepsiades' creditors in *Clouds*. He was not, however, a professional moneylender but a notorious effeminate and wastrel, probably addicted to gambling.

ANDROKLES: A homosexual.

ANTIPHON: A parasite and starveling.

APOLLO: God of prophecy, music, healing, and light; his two chief shrines were at Delphoi (q.v.) and the island of Delos (q.v.).

ARIGNOTOS: An excellent harper and a friend of Aristophanes.

ARIPHRADES: Son of Automenes and a notorious pervert. Indeed, his perversities (cunnilingual and perhaps worse still) seem to have struck Aristophanes as an altogether novel form of sexual self-expression.

ARTEMIS: Goddess of the hunt and the moon, sister of Apollo (q.v.).

ASKLEPIOS: Son of Apollo; god of medicine.

ASKONDAS: A contender against Ephoudion (q.v.) at the Olympic games; otherwise unknown.

ATHENA, ATHENE: Goddess of wisdom and war and patroness of Athens. On her breast she wore the *aegis,* a goatskin plated with scales and a Gorgon's head in the center.

BRASIDAS: Distinguished Spartan general of the Peloponnesian War, particularly famed for his victories in Thrace and his defeat of Kleon.

BYZANTION: A city on the Bosporus and a subject-city of the Athenian Empire. Its siege by the Athenians under Kimon in 469 was celebrated.

CHABES: An old juror, crony of Philokleon.

CHAIREPHON: A pupil and disciple of Sokrates; his scrawniness and emaciated pallor are constantly ridiculed by Aristophanes.

CHAIREAS: A man whose claim to fame was his son, a notorious pervert who was not even, according to the Scholiast, an Athenian citizen.

CHARINADES: An old juror, crony of Philokleon.

DELOS: Small Aegean island sacred to Apollo.

DELPHOI, DELPHI: A town in Phokis, celebrated for its great temple and oracle of Apollo.

DEMETER: The Earth-Mother; goddess of grain, agriculture, and the harvest, worshipped in her shrine at Eleusis in Attika.

DEMOS: In this play, not Demos, the personified populace of Athens, but Demos, the son of Pyrilampes, noted for stupidity and effeminacy, a victim of the pun in his name.

DERKYLOS: A drunkard.

DIONYSOS: God of vineyards, wine, and dramatic poetry; also called Bacchos, Evios, Bromios, etc.

DRAKONTIDES: His identity is uncertain, but he was probably a member of the oligarchical party and perhaps one of those who preferred charges against Perikles.

EKBATANA: A city in Media, once the capital of the Median Kingdom, and later the summer residence of the Persian kings. For the average Greek, Ekbatana was a kind of El Dorado, a distant city of fabulous wealth.

EPHOUDION: Victor in pankration (mixed wrestling and boxing) at Olympia in 464 B.C.

ERGASION: Evidently a farmer; otherwise unknown.

EUATHLOS: An orator and informer of no principles; it was he who brought charges against Perikles' rival, Thoukydides (q.v.), after his return from ostracism.

EUBOIA: A large and fertile island northeast of Attika. In 445 Perikles planted an Athenian colony on the island and otherwise exploited it. As a result the island revolted and had to be resubjugated. This time, however, Perikles' treatment of the island was so severe that it was commonly said (at least by his enemies) that he had "stretched Euboia on the rack of torture."

EUERGIDES: An old juror, otherwise unknown.

EUPHEMIOS: A boon-companion of Theoros (q.v.) and perhaps, like him, a demagogic orator. Nothing else is known about him, though given the context in which his name appears (*Wasps,* 599), it seems clear that nothing *good* could have been known.

EURIPIDES: Athenian tragedian (480-406 B.C.) whose character and plays were constantly ridiculed by Aristophanes. Euripides' mother may have been (though this is uncertain) a marketwoman who sold chervil, and Aristophanes never tires of twitting the tragedian about his mother's vegetables.

EURYKLES: A prophet who claimed to be possessed and thus to have the power to speak through the mouths of others.

HARMODIOS: Murderer of the tyrant Hippias (q.v.) and much honored in Athens; a famous drinking song records the tyrannicide.

HEKATE: Goddess of the moon, night, childbirth, and the underworld. At Athens a small shrine of Hekate was set up in the vestibule of every house.

HELLESPONT: Strait which divides Asia Minor from Thrace.

HERAKLES: Hero and demigod, son of Zeus and Alkmene; renowned for his great labors, his prodigious strength, and his gluttonous appetite.

HESTIA: Goddess of the hearth.

HIPPIAS: Athenian tyrant of the sixth century, murdered by Harmodios (q.v.) and Aristogeiton.

HIPPYLLOS: A debauchee; otherwise unknown.

INO: Euripidean heroine-in-tatters and wife of Athamas. She threw herself at her mad husband's feet, begging for mercy, but he refused to listen and threw her into the sea where she was transformed into the sea-goddess Leukothea.

KARDOPION: A semicomic name (it means "Little Kneading-Trough") used as a matter of convention in telling a certain kind of story (compare, for instance, "Little Audrey").

KARKINOS: An Athenian tragic poet whose poetry and three sons are all ridiculed by Aristophanes. Karkinos' name means "Crab."

KEKROPS, CECROPS: Legendary first king of Attika and reputed founder of Athens. Hence "country of Kekrops" is equivalent to "Athens," and "son of Kekrops" to "Athenian." He is usually represented as twiform, i.e., with the head and upper trunk of a man, but serpent-shaped below (symbolizing his earthborn origin).

KLEISTHENES: A notorious homosexual, and one of Aristophanes' favorite targets.

KLEON: Son of Kleinetos; the most notorious and powerful of all Athenian demagogues. After the death of Perikles in 429 B.C., Kleon became, until his own death in 422, the leader of the radical democracy and the anti-Spartan extremists in Athens. An impressive speaker and a thoroughly unscrupulous and venal politician, he was bitterly loathed and attacked by Aristophanes. In 424 B.C., thanks to his coup in capturing the Spartan hoplites at Sphakteria, he reached the height of his power; so unchallengeable was his position that he was able to persuade the Athenians not to accept the handsome terms offered by Sparta in an attempt to recover her imprisoned hoplites. Filled with confidence in his military ability and tempted by the hope of further glory, Kleon took command of an Athenian army in Thrace, where, in 422, he was defeated and killed by the Spartan forces under Brasidas (q.v.).

In Aristophanes' *Knights,* Kleon is only slightly masked under the name of Paphlagon.

KLEONYMOS: A corpulent glutton and part-time informer; Aristophanes' commonest butt for cowardice (i.e., throwing one's shield away).

KORYBANTES: Frenzied priests of the goddess Kybele (the Phrygian Earth-mother whose worship was ecstatic and orgiastic).

KRONOS: Father of Zeus, Hera, and Poseidon. Deprived of his rule by Zeus. Synonymous with "old fogy."

KYDATHENEA: An Athenian deme; the birthplace of Kleon and Aristophanes.

LACHES: An Athenian general, defeated in Sicily in 427 B.C.; in 424 he besieged Delion, and may have been prosecuted by Kleon for peculation in Sicily.

LASOS: Of Hermione, a lyric poet.

LEOGORAS: A wealthy Athenian gourmet, addicted to horse-raising (or possibly to pheasant-breeding). Father of the orator Andokides.

LYDIA: A district of Asia Minor; under its greatest king, Kroisos (Croesus), it included almost all of Asia Minor from the river Halys to the Ionian coast. Its wealth and effeminacy were proverbial among Greeks.

LYKON: A debauchee; otherwise unknown.

LYKOS: Legendary son of Pandion and patron of jurors.

LYKINOS: A name; otherwise unknown.

LYSISTRATOS: An acid-tongued demagogue, evidently a starveling and a parasite.

MARATHON: The famous battle (490 B.C.) in which the Athenian forces under Miltiades crushingly defeated the first Persian invasion of Hellas.

MEGARA: The Greek state to the west of Attika. Subject first to the boycott imposed by Perikles' Megarian Decree (432 B.C.) and later to frequent Athenian incursions, plus the inroads of the Peloponnesian forces on their way to ravage Attika in the winters, it was reduced quite early in the war to extreme hunger and poverty.

MIDAS: A Phrygian slave.

MORYCHOS: A noted Athenian epicure and dandy.

NAXOS: An island in the Aegean, conquered by the Athenians under Kimon, probably about 468 B.C.

NIKOSTRATOS: A superstitious religious fanatic.

NIOBE: Mythical daughter of Tantalos, proud mother of six sons and six daughters, all slain by Artemis and Apollo because Niobe boasted herself to be better than Leto. The subject of tragedies by Aischylos and Sophokles.

ODEION: A covered theater in Athens which also did service as a lawcourt.

ODYSSEUS: King of Ithaka and hero of the Trojan War; renowned for his resourcefulness and cunning.

OIAGROS: An Athenian tragic actor.

OLYMPIA: A plain in Elis where the Olympic Games were celebrated.

PAIAN: Manifestation of Apollo as god of healing.

PARNASSOS: A high mountain to the north of Delphoi (q.v.); one of the chief haunts of Apollo and the Muses, but frequented also by Dionysos.

PAROS: An island in the Aegean, a site of a disastrous expedition under Miltiades in 489 B.C.

PHANOS: A henchman of Kleon, who seems to have lent his name to suits and investigations instigated by Kleon.

PHAYLLOS: A famous runner.

PHILIPPOS: An orator, amateur sophist, and informer.

PHILOKTEMON: According to the Scholiast, a glutton and drunkard, famous for keeping perpetual Open House.

PHILOXENOS: A pervert.

PHLYA: An Athenian deme.

PHRYGIA: A region of Asia Minor, once ruled by the Lydians and then incorporated into the Persian Empire. It was particularly prone to a kind of religion marked by frenzy and ecstatic excess, familiar to Greece in the worship of Kybele and the Phrygian Dionysos.

PHRYNICHOS: (1) An early Athenian tragedian, an older contemporary of Aischylos. (2) A tragic actor and dancer, contemporary with Aristophanes.

POSEIDON: Brother of Zeus and god of the sea. As god of the sea, he girdles the earth and has it in his power, as Poseidon the Earth-shaker, to cause earthquakes. In still another manifestation, he is Poseidon Hippios, patron god of horses and horsemen.

PROXENIDES: A notorious braggart and liar.

SAMOS: A large Aegean island lying off the coast of Ionia. It was a member state of the Athenian Confederacy until 440 B.C. when it revolted. The islanders resisted for a heroic nine months against the Athenians dispatched to reconquer it.

SARDIS: One-time capital of the kingdom of Lydia; under the Persians the residence of the satrap of Lydia. Ever since the time of Kroisos (Croesus), Greeks had regarded Sardis as a place of fabulous wealth and the frequent embassies sent there confirmed the reports.

SIMONIDES: Of Keos, the great sixth-century lyric poet.

SKIONE: A town situated on the peninsula of Pallene (cf. CHALKIDIKE). After it revolted from the Athenian Empire, the Athenians were forced to spend several months of extremely bitter winter weather in blockading it.

SOLON: Famous Athenian legislator (ca. 638-558 B.C.), whose achievement it was to have ended debt slavery in Athens.

SOSIAS: A common servile name.

STHENELOS: A vulgar, third-rate tragic poet.

STRYMODOROS: An old juror, crony of Philokleon.

SYBARIS: A famous and proverbially wealthy Greek city in Lucania, completely destroyed by the inhabitants of Kroton in 510 B.C. A Sybaris story was a fable which, unlike the fables of Aesop, used men rather than animals as characters.

THEOGENES: An Athenian braggart and beggar.

THEOPHRASTOS: A debauchee; otherwise unknown.

THEOROS: Flatterer, perjuror, sycophant of Kleon.

THESPIS: Poet, regarded by the ancients as the creator of tragedy (fl. 534 B.C.)

THESSALY: A large district in northern Greece.

THOUKYDIDES: Son of Melesias; not to be confused with the historian Thoukydides, son of Oloros. Leader of the conservative and anti-imperialistic party in opposition to Perikles. In 443 he was ostracized; when in 433 he returned to Athens, he was involved in a ruinous lawsuit on the charges of Euathlos (q.v.).

THRACE: The eastern half of the Balkan peninsula.

THRATTA: A Thracian woman; i.e., a common name for a female domestic slave of Thracian origins.

XANTHIAS: A common servile name.

ZEUS: Chief god of the Olympian pantheon; son of Kronos, brother of Poseidon, and father of Athena. As the supreme ruler of the world, he is armed with thunder and lightning and creates storms and tempests.